EDUCATION FOR A DEVELOPING REGION

by the same author

THE NEW SOCIETIES OF TROPICAL AFRICA

STUDIES IN MANAGEMENT

EDUCATION FOR
A DEVELOPING
REGION

A Study in East Africa

BY

GUY HUNTER

Political and Economic
Planning

The Institute of Race
Relations

GEORGE ALLEN AND UNWIN LTD
LONDON

PRINTED IN GREAT BRITAIN
in 10 point Baskerville type
BY R. J. ACFORD LTD
CHICHESTER

PREFACE

This study of educational opportunity in East Africa represents the first section of a larger research project undertaken by P.E.P. with the aid of a grant from the Ford Foundation. The main purpose of the entire project is to analyse the conditions which overseas students (particularly Africans) meet during their studies in the United Kingdom; the degree to which the courses they attend fulfil their needs and expectations; and some of the difficulties involved in providing a bigger flow of British teachers to overseas countries.

It was clear that work in the United Kingdom could only be intelligently done if there were a full understanding of the needs and motives which bring students to this country, and of the still-existing gaps in educational and training opportunities overseas. It was therefore part of the original project to include a study of at least one major area of Africa as a sample case.

It happened that Mr Guy Hunter of the Institute of Race Relations was engaged in a manpower assessment in East Africa during the summer of 1962. This involved an investigation of the output from secondary schools, the university colleges, and a variety of vocational and technical training schemes in the area. The Institute therefore agreed that Mr Hunter should extend his work in East Africa, with a somewhat different emphasis, so as to provide this first section of the whole project. The Institute has a special interest, in that the training of manpower to staff the developing East African countries depends greatly upon the full use of the resources of all races—European and Asian as well as African. Part of the research grant was therefore made available to the Institute, and the resulting study is sponsored jointly by P.E.P. and the Institute of Race Relations. The second part of the research is being carried out in the United Kingdom by P.E.P. and the result will be published as a companion volume in 1964. Both P.E.P. and the Institute of Race Relations would like to acknowledge the help and encouragement given to this project by the Department of Technical Co-operation.

P.E.P.
I.R.R.

Author's Acknowledgements

I would like to record my great gratitude to the staff of the Departments in East Africa, who took much trouble and time to give us accurate information, and to the staff of many other Departments and of business firms who contributed material on training. I would also like to thank the large number of Headmasters and Principals whom we visited, often with the shortest of notice or none at all, and who gave us so much of their time and hospitality. I was most fortunate in having my wife as a fellow-worker and, as usual, this book owes a great deal of its content to her faithful notes of endless facts and figures obtained in interviews and to her suggestions and criticisms. I am most grateful also to the editor and staff of the Institute of Race Relations who put the manuscript into final shape.

G.H.

May 1963

CONTENTS

		PAGE
PREFACE		V
INTRODUCTION		ix

PART I   THE GROWTH OF EDUCATION AND TRAINING IN EAST AFRICA

I	*The Early Development of African Education*	3
II	*Asian and European Education*	17
III	*The Present Facts*	
	1. *The Schools*	23
	2. *Technical Education and Industrial Training*	28
	3. *Government Vocational Training*	35
	4. *University Opportunity*	38
	Appendix I	44

PART II   POLICY ISSUES

IV	*The Public Need—Manpower Requirements*	57
V	*The Public Need—Supply from Education and Training*	63
VI	*The Public Need—The Case for Overseas Training*	70
VII	*Scholarship Programmes and Problems*	81
	Appendix II. Bursaries, Scholarships and Loans for Higher Education	92
VIII	*Private Ambitions and Incentives*	97
IX	*Conclusions—Some Policy Issues*	106
	Index	114

INTRODUCTION

This Study of education and training in Kenya, Uganda and Tanganyika is written with the closest reference to the circumstances and ambitions of these countries as they come forward to take their place as modern independent nations. It might therefore be accused of treating education simply as a tool of political and social purpose or economic need. Such a tool it is, at least in one dimension, and has been in all ages and societies. In the simplest tribal groups education prepares the child to enter smoothly into the adult world, training him in family, social, religious and military obligations, as well as in productive crafts. In advanced societies the learning of techniques will bulk larger, but moral and social training also play a great part. But there is another dimension of education, which is concerned with the development of the individual, and which, taking for granted the need for social and technical training, seeks to open out for the single human being the full potentialities of his personality and talents.

Little is said here on this personal level, although it touches the deepest issues and offers to the working teacher the main reward of his vocation. But there need be no clash between the social and personal approach if indeed concern for the individual is a dimension, and not a separate field, of an education which must in any case be shaped to a real society in some particular time and place and circumstance. We are not concerned with Erewhon, but with East Africa in 1963.

And, in all conscience, the challenge of social and technical purpose, in Africa and in many other developing countries, is so revolutionary that perhaps the first priority is to establish a structure fit to meet it; without that the individual will find no firm standing ground from which to develop his personal quality. If the purpose of education is 'to reproduce the type and provide for growth beyond the type',[1] it is the second half of this definition, the more dynamic half, which at present is in issue. The task is not to reproduce the old African society but to create, in a generation, a new one—new in language, custom, skills, political and social relationships; new in attitudes and responsibilities and beliefs. It is certainly not enough to produce skills, of pharmacy or engineering; leadership, tolerance, self-discipline, obedience to the truth, a conscience relevant to new roles and temptations—all these are equally needed. If this book deals mainly with structure and administration,

[1] W. E. Hocking.

ix

examinations and scholarships, it is not because those needs have been forgotten. Rather, they have been assumed.

The immediate purpose of this book is to examine the opportunities for education and training which are open to East Africans in their own country, with some indication of the gaps and deficiencies which might be filled by sending students overseas. Obviously it must take into account the political and economic objectives of African governments; but there is also a pressure from the demand side—from students (and their parents) determined to find entry into secondary schools, or to continue education after secondary school. For it is these pressures, which of course affect government plans, which create some of the most controversial problems in education for all developing countries. In the background is a further financial issue—the amount of money which can be devoted to education as against other forms of investment in countries with limited resources and heavy claims upon them. This issue would need a thorough economic analysis beyond the scope of this book, and I have contented myself with mentioning, at certain points, the arguments for economical rather than expensive ways of meeting needs, because such arguments must be given weight.

It must be clear, then, that this short book does not cover the whole vast range of educational problems—syllabus and method, philosophy and psychology—nor even the full relationship between education and development. It is concerned with the needs as seen by governments anxious to staff a new society; with the pressure from individuals anxious to equip themselves for modern life; and with some of the problems of structure, standards, and finance which arise from these two main sources. As this book was going to press, Professor Adam Curle published his stimulating study of *Educational Strategy for Developing Societies*.[1] This study does not pretend to any such wide range and generality; it is primarily a detailed case study of the actual day-to-day problems of educational policy in a particular area—the stubborn facts from which wider strategy must be planned.

In broad outline, the problems arise at two levels, and to some extent in sequence. The new and intense pressure for primary education continued right through to completion of the primary course means that during the next four or five years there will be a staggering rate of increase in the numbers emerging from primary schools with a pass in their final examination. In consequence, it will almost certainly be impossible to find places in secondary schools for even 10 per cent of primary leavers; the percentage may go down to 6 per cent despite all efforts to expand secondary

[1] (London, Tavistock Publications, 1963.)

education quickly. The financial problem is unavoidable; every extra £1,000 spent on expanding primary either means £1,000 less for secondary (which would narrow the bottleneck still further), or a further increase of educational against other investment. The educational problem admits of a wider choice of policy. The danger is of expanding secondary schools so fast that their quality is lost in the process; this in turn produces a crisis at the level of university entrance, with the danger of pulling university standards down. That this danger is real could be evidenced by the melancholy sequence of events in Burma and to some degree in Eastern Nigeria. The alternative of retaining a narrow post-primary bottleneck is probably politically impossible, or will be in East Africa within two or three years. It is probable that an alternative form of less academic secondary school will have to be introduced, whatever its title; 'comprehensive' schools are one possibility.

The next crisis is bound to follow, one stage higher up. The great increase in secondary leavers at Form 4 (School Certificate or GCE(O)) will in due course produce violent pressure partly on Sixth Forms but more strongly for some post-secondary 'college' education entered from Form 4 and demanding a less academic, more practical syllabus. East Africa has scarcely felt this pressure as yet, because the output from Form 4 has barely sufficed to provide both an entry to Sixth Forms and an adequate recruitment for the many forms of post-secondary vocational training—teachers, central government, agricultural and medical services, industry. But within three years at most supply will have caught up. Although the top level of secondary leavers will still have no difficulty in finding Sixth Form and university places, and although opportunity for other post-secondary training should still be good, the prestige of a university Degree and the knowledge that many universities in foreign countries admit students with eleven (and sometimes ten) years of education will build up a vociferous demand from secondary leavers for immediate university entrance.

The pro's and con's of this argument are dealt with in some detail in chapter VI. But it is worth asking bluntly whether it is better to be in the position which East Africa and perhaps Malaya are reaching, with a small stream entering high quality universities and considerable political pressure from the disappointed candidates; or to be in the position already reached by Burma, Indonesia, Philippines, where great numbers are entering universities with much lower standards and great numbers of poorly qualified graduates are unemployed, or taking jobs as clerks, or seeking, not always successfully, to get some post-graduate qualification overseas in order to earn a qualification which will carry conviction with an employer. These are the extreme positions; there could be a midway course, retaining the quality of both grammar schools and principal universities, by providing, possibly in sequence, alternative outlets both at secondary and at post-secondary level. It may be that Nigeria and Ghana are finding this middle path.

This is by no means an academic problem; for in Central Africa in particular the main issue still lies ahead. Northern Rhodesia and Nyasaland are launching into self-government with a Sixth Form system, no university of their own, and an immense demand for Africans to replace Europeans in the whole range of public service. Some difficult decisions will have to be taken, with an eye to the future as well as the present, and the precedent of East African policy is sure to be carefully watched.

It is a question which also deeply affects the relation between East African education and the flow of students to Great Britain. Admission qualifications into existing United Kingdom universities are not likely to be lowered, either for undergraduate or post-graduate work. If Africans cannot offer Higher School Certificate or at least a suitable GCE(A), the door will be closed, and the pressure for preliminary study in Britain from Form 4, to reach university entrance, will rise. This is unsatisfactory and expensive; the alternative would be for Africans who go abroad to go only to those foreign universities which admit at Form 4 level. Further, any serious fall in East African university standards would make it increasingly difficult to recruit British university staff, who might well be unwilling to risk their future academic career by accepting overseas posts in institutions with Form 4 entry. In the long run, if the United Kingdom system remains rigidly in its present shape, and if the pressure for larger more generalized university education with a lower entry point proves victorious overseas, the result could be to cut many of the links between this country and the developing nations, including the new Commonwealth countries, who would look increasingly to the more flexible systems of other foreign nations.

This issue has been clouded by a good deal of emotion, and accusations of educational snobbery have been thrown at the Sixth Form system and the attitude of British universities. But standards in certain fields at least are real, as many countries who relaxed them have found to their cost. There are certain mathematical techniques which are needed for some technologies; there is a degree of precision and clarity required for the social sciences if they are not to wallow in the verbosity and tautology which characterize much second-rate sociology today. These things are not to be blown away by striking emotional attitudes.

A more serious issue has been raised by those who say that Africa or South-East Asia does not need the levels of scholarship or attainment required in developed countries; that men of good general education, in large numbers, to carry out fairly simple tasks of development are needed and needed quickly, and that they can be provided without so much academic pother. There is clearly more than a grain of truth in this argument, though it is not the whole truth. For, as developing countries are well aware, they cannot close their frontiers to the outer world and develop systems, either of economics or of education, which are purely local. Indeed, their anxiety to 'catch up', to achieve quite new technical and social standards, is itself a drive for more, and not less, integration with the technical and the administrative standards of the modern international world. It may well be that each country can and should develop a range of intermediate institutions suited to the urgency and size of its needs. But few would deny the need to keep at least a life line in contact with the best levels of international thought and achievement; and to do so certainly involves maintaining at least some local institutions of the highest quality.

For the sake of clarity, these issues have here been put in sharper contrast than they are actually felt. It may be worth while to add that, even within the last few months, there are signs in England of much anxiety for the health of our own non-university system, with its roots in the secondary modern school. This concern is not likely to attack the older university standards as such. But it may well draw increasing attention to the distortions which the prestige of grammar school and university is producing among the vast majority of British boys and girls who in fact never enter this top layer. This new thinking might well lead to experiments with a new type of 'college' education, more broadly and practically based. If so, it would certainly lead to a greater sympathy with the problems of developing countries in this very field and to renewed possibilities of co-operation with them.

These problems of the type and standard of higher education which is going to be needed and acceptable in East Africa lie at the heart of the detailed discussion of scholarships and overseas aid with which the remainder of this book is concerned. Perhaps more emphasis should be laid on 'type', because 'standard' is an ambiguous word, and a word which too quickly acquires emotional significance. Every type of education, including primary, can have its own high 'standard', in the sense of quality. Technical education can also be of high standard in another sense, of teaching extremely advanced applied techniques. University education, at least as seen through British eyes, has its own and different excellence. In technological fields it may well turn out students much less able to handle applied work immediately than the student who has come through apprenticeship and technical college. Education good of its type would be a closer definition of aim.

In fact these confusions have greatly helped to bedevil education in almost all developing countries by building up the immense prestige of the university as 'the best'. Experience in Africa and elsewhere leads to two major conclusions, which may be worth stating, however risky such generalizations are. First, there almost always develops an acute shortage of technicians—from shorthand typists[1] to a man able to blow glass in a laboratory or maintain aircraft instruments. This happens largely because the prestige of the university has deflected both student ambitions and government attention (and teachers and money) away from the essential technical institutions. The account of technical education in East Africa in chapter III bears this out—and East Africa has done better, particularly in departmental extension and technical training, than most other countries. Shortage of technicians is almost a routine conclusion of any Manpower Survey in any part of the developing world.

The second conclusion is harder to prove but, in my belief, yet more important. It is, in those fields where university education is most relevant, the need for the very highest quality. I have here particularly in mind the senior administrators. In country after country where the State has undertaken the major responsibility for development, splendid paper plans grind slowly to frustration and even failure because of the fog of words, slips in the cogs of administration, inaccurate statistics, slipshod thinking, bad evaluation of priorities. Here and there will be found one first-rate administrator, bowed down by overwork and over-haste, trying desperately to cut his way through. But his feet are held in the mud, because too many of his colleagues and supporters have not learned, because their university did not teach them, the honesty and precision of thought, the ability to look past the larger abstract phrase to the concrete situation, which are hall-marks of a well trained mind. In the days when major decisions of policy were taken from outside, it was easy to suppose that high academic standards were unnecessary, and that Permanent Secretaries were overpaid. But if the developing countries, on their own, are to develop the momentum and the firm grip on the huge administrative problems which they have set themselves, they need, not a huge number of mass-produced graduates, but a much smaller number of men of the highest quality, supported by technicians who are not ashamed of their calling. It is in these two fields that Britain can offer most to East Africa.

Ever since the Ashby Report in Nigeria, the air has been full of ambitious recommendations for massive educational advance in developing countries. Inspiring visions, involving immense financial expenditure, have been put forward for country after country; and

---

[1] Dr Nyerere is reported to have cried 'My kingdom for twenty good stenographers'.

the gale of popular desire blows behind these schemes. The argument is that 'underdevelopment' is in essence due to lack of education more than to any other single cause. This argument is in a sense true. But there are dangerous ambiguities in it—about the nature of education and in the distinction between the causes of underdevelopment and the processes necessary to cure it. Calculations about the percentage of *total population* which should have secondary or university education are apt to forget that, at present, this type of education is suited to the *modern sector*, which may represent only a third or a tenth of the whole society. For example, President Sukarno has announced a target of 1,000,000 university students to match the 100,000,000 Indonesian population. But the modern sector of Indonesia is probably not as large as that of Ghana, with 7,000,000 population. To give a modern sector education to far more young men than can find a modern job is to create a growing mass of 'frustrated graduates' who cannot find work to match their new abilities and are invariably unwilling to look for it in the rural subsistence economy. On the other hand, to deny education to all but the small group needed for the modern sector would be equally if not more disastrous. It is clear that two types of education are needed, the one to bring forward the whole rural society on a broad front, the other to create a right proportion of modern skills. The balance of these two must shift in time with a quite different process—the rate of growth of the 'modern sector' within the whole economy. How to maintain this balance rightly is the great question of educational strategy.

Before turning to the detailed examination of facts and figures and day-to-day problems in East Africa, with which this book is mainly concerned, it would be wrong to omit, as a subject of major emphasis, the complications which racial feeling could—and, alas, already does—add to the scene. Granted the fact of political independence, already existing or, in Kenya, soon to come, it would be futile to question African anxiety to replace at least the majority of Europeans in the public posts which influence policy. This replacement is already far advanced, and the training and manpower planning to continue it is already in hand. Rather different arguments may well apply to European technologists in the economic fields, to teachers, and perhaps to European agriculture in Kenya—narrower political motives are here balanced by economic and social arguments of great weight.

But the situation between the African majority and the Asian minority is on a very different footing. The Asian community has never been a ruling group, and no political threat comes from it. Nor, in the main, is it a landlord class; nor, thanks to government credit schemes, restrictive legislation, and the wide spread of

Co-operatives, is it heavily involved in money-lending to farmers against future crops. Thus most of the animosity which can develop against a 'Bania' class is not applicable to Asians. They have been, indeed, the wholesalers and retailers of East Africa, both in towns and in the bush, and have constantly been accused of exploiting the African customer. Whether this accusation is better founded than the grumbles against middlemen all over the world would need extremely careful study. The other main grudge of Africans against Asians is that Asians, with a longer tradition of craft, commercial and clerical skills, have occupied just that middle level of technical, clerical and administrative posts to which tens of thousands of African school leavers now aspire. In a word, there is jealousy which can be focused on an 'other' group which is distinguishable by physique and culture, a culture not native to the African continent. This is plain, straightforward racialism, however it is disguised or rationalized. It is directed vaguely against all who came from the Indian sub-continent, Pakistanis and Indians, Gujaratis and Goans, Sikhs, Muslims and Hindus.

This feeling is highly relevant to the education and manpower needs of East Africa. As the figures in chapter IV show (and they are rough figures, but the best so far obtainable), Asians represented in 1961 45 per cent of all the top-level manpower available to run the East African economies and public services, although the bulk of this figure represents the technician as against technologist category. Asians are dominant in the commercial economy and provide also a heavy share of the professional cadres—engineers, lawyers, doctors, accountants. Any wholesale attack on their opportunity to hold responsible positions, whether in commerce or the public service, would accentuate the existing manpower emergency in East Africa and cripple a large section of commerce and trade. The sympathy and help which Britain can and does offer in aiding African education and manpower needs would be much tempered if those needs were doubled by a large-scale programme of racial discrimination; our own past guilt in this matter will make us more rather than less critical of the same failings in others. As it is, at least some of our help, and perhaps an increased share of it, ought to be going to Asian students, whose educational and above all career opportunities in East Africa are already severely reduced and may be reduced much further. Despite the hostility which too many local Europeans have shown towards the Asian groups in East Africa, they have contributed greatly to the growth of East African economies and will continue to do so if they are allowed even a reasonable opportunity to play their part.

PART I

THE GROWTH OF EDUCATION
AND TRAINING IN EAST AFRICA

CHAPTER I

THE EARLY DEVELOPMENT OF
AFRICAN EDUCATION

I. INTRODUCTORY—THE SCHOOL SYSTEM

The reader who is not thoroughly familiar with East African education may like to have a few very simple definitions at the outset.

The school system on the African side consists essentially, in Kenya and in Tanganyika, of an eight-year primary system (Standards I to VIII); there is usually a break at Standard IV, and Standards V to VIII have been called 'intermediate' (Kenya) or 'middle schools' (Tanganyika). This eight-year *primary* course, which may very soon be reduced to a seven-year course, is followed by a four-year *secondary* course, Forms 1 to 4. In an increasing, but still small number of schools a further two years of secondary education is given in Forms 5 and 6. The main examinations come at the end of the primary course (Standard VIII), at Form 4, when Cambridge Overseas School Certificate is taken, and at Form 6, when Higher School Certificate may be taken.

There is a variation in Uganda, where at Standard VI in the primary course pupils go on to two years[1] in a 'junior secondary' school, before entering the secondary school proper in the ninth year of education, as in the other two countries. The term 'secondary' will only be used for this course starting in the ninth year at Form 1, in all countries. 'Primary' will be used to *include* 'junior secondary' in Uganda—i.e. up to and including the eighth year.

Almost all African secondary schools are residential, but some day secondary schools are now being established. Further, African pupils are now being admitted to what were Asian day secondary schools, mainly in large towns.

African primary schools for boys are almost wholly staffed by African teachers. The secondary schools, and most African girls' schools, are still heavily dependent upon expatriate teachers.

[1] Those who did not secure entry into secondary schools used to do a third year in junior secondary. This system has now been abolished.

3

The Asian school system, now being 'integrated' (though slowly) with the African, has until now consisted normally of a six- or seven-year primary course followed by a six-year secondary course reaching Form 6. The schools are almost entirely staffed by Asian teachers, though a very few African teachers are now coming in.

The European system was based upon a variety of primary and private schools, followed (except in Uganda) by what were roughly 'public schools'—five major schools in Kenya and one in Tanganyika (which is likely to close).

SUMMARY

	PRIMARY	SECONDARY
African	Standards I–IV	
	Standards V–VIII (middle: intermediate)	Forms 1 to 4 (School Certificate)
	or VII–VIII (junior— secondary, Uganda)	Forms 5 and 6 (Higher School Certificate)
Asian	Standards I–VI or VII	As for African
European	Standards I–VI	As for African

The great variety of technical and other types of education will be mentioned, where necessary, in the following chapters.

2. LEGACIES FROM THE PAST—LANGUAGE

It is not necessary for the present purpose to trace in any detail the growth of education in East Africa, save in so far as early policies have left a mark on the situation today. There are perhaps three respects in which this legacy is important. The first relates to the use of a vernacular, Kiswahili or English in the schools; the second is the main type of syllabus adopted; the third is the quality of environment, equipment and teaching.

Until 1961, it was the policy that in the first years of primary school the language of instruction should be the local vernacular. English, and to some extent Kiswahili, were taught as foreign languages, and English only became effectively the language of instruction in the fourth or fifth year of education. There were both educational and practical reasons for this decision. Educationally it was believed that intellectual and emotional growth might be stunted if in the earliest years of education language departed from the language of the home, where its words carried so strong an emotional content. Much was written on this subject in the years after the War during the various reviews of African education. In particular, the Binns Report to the Nuffield Foundation examined the arguments on both sides.

The practical arguments probably weighed even more heavily. In the early days African primary teachers, the great majority of whom had left school at the end of an eight-year course, followed by two years in a teacher training college, would not have been able to teach in English; and it was felt necessary to postpone the effective introduction of English to the last four years of primary education— Standards V to VIII where a higher standard of teaching could be maintained.

The fact that Africans entered secondary education with only four or five years of English behind them (and that taught and used only moderately by African teachers) meant not only that the English examination in Cambridge Overseas School Certificate was and still is by far the most frequent cause of failure; it meant that by Standard VIII, and probably even after four years in secondary school, most African pupils were mentally translating what they were taught from English back to a vernacular, and what they said or wrote from the vernacular into English. They had, of course, been taught to translate; for in the first years of school they were being taught 'Western' concepts in the vernacular, and therefore acquired *a vernacular vocabulary for school subjects* which they were likely to go on using even when English became the teaching medium. In consequence, the ability to think in English was long delayed, if ever acquired. It is easy to see why African pupils became so devoted to the text book and so much better on paper (where there is time to translate) than in oral response.

This language problem—complicated further by learning Kiswahili—not only results in able boys failing to get a high pass in School Certificate owing to failure in English, thus narrowing the stream considered eligible for Sixth Form work and eventual entry to the university. It also accentuates the vital role of Sixth Forms, where many pupils pass for the first time from absorbing instruction and texts to thinking for themselves. It also no doubt accounts for the observation, so frequently made by expatriate employers, that 'Africans' perform well within the bounds of the knowledge they have actually been taught but seem slow to transfer the principles underlying that knowledge to new situations or problems, in which the elements of their knowledge have to be recombined in new ways.

These issues will reappear later as elements in several important policy decisions. However, as from 1961 an experiment in the teaching of English as from Standard I has been introduced. The first results (in over fifty schools in Kenya in 1962) appear at first sight greatly encouraging, and the system is to be widely extended. If in fact it results in making English the natural language for thought and expression of Western knowledge and concepts, it may go far to bring the African educational system more into line with international standards, and thereby speed up the production of fully qualified men from local institutions with far less reliance on overseas scholarships.

3. LEGACIES—THE SYLLABUS

It has been constantly stated, and not only in relation to Africa, that the British introduced a far too 'literary' and 'academic' type of schooling to their dependencies; and it is further alleged that this syllabus was biased towards white collar occupations, and against the practical needs of a population bound to be mainly concerned with a rural, agricultural life. In so far as this is true, it is of importance at this moment when Africans are seeking to obtain quickly the practical skills of the West, and particularly the knowledge and attitudes required for modernizing agriculture.

In many ways this accusation is wrongly framed. Early Mission education was of course first concerned with sheer literacy, at a low level for the mass and a rather higher level for those pupils who could be made into simple teachers to spread education, in their own language, further into the 'bush'. But even in the early stages many Missions, particularly the Catholics in East Africa,[1] were almost equally bent on teaching practical crafts, so that their growing communities could build their own class rooms and chapels and grow much of their own food; and this tradition of practical work is still quite strong in many schools.

Nevertheless, the British tradition of education is essentially humanistic,[2] designed to give, or enable the child to acquire, a sight of the fundamental values upon which Western civilization is based. These values are enshrined, naturally, in religion, literature and history and in the enquiring spirit of science. The schools of England were not primarily concerned to teach practical skills, which were quickly and necessarily learned by a child in a hard-working environment or acquired by subsequent training. They were designed to give literacy, in both the arts and the elements of mathematics and science, so that the child of working parents could eventually look beyond the narrow limits of his life and of purely traditional skills to a wider world of ideas and a more modern technical competence. The British child grew up in a home and public environment which at least nominally accepted the same values and used the same language and concepts as were taught in school.

[1] See particularly Roland Oliver, *The Missionary Factor in East Africa* (London, Longmans, 1952).

[2] See particularly article by P. C. C. Evans, 'Western Education and Rural Productivity in Tropical Africa' (*Africa*, Vol. XXXII, No. 4, October 1962). This article deals admirably with this whole subject.

Applied in Africa, this system was surrounded by an African world which neither knew the values nor used the skills and concepts in daily life. It was natural enough to concentrate upon the tools of literacy, particularly reading, so that the African child could begin to reach some vision of a world of values and methods wholly outside his own. Moreover, for purely practical reasons, the colonisers needed Africans to help in the lower levels of teaching, administration and construction—teachers, clerks, masons and carpenters were in demand. But methods of agriculture were embedded in African custom and indeed the whole nexus of religion, kinship and social order. It would have been impossible for the early schools to make much impact on this, even if the teachers had been competent or felt it their business to do so.

While at first the European system of values and schooling was often violently rejected or neglected, a time came when Africans suddenly saw in it their salvation, both from their poverty and from their 'inferiority' to the developed nations. They contrasted, however inarticulately, a world of illiterate, custom-bound subsistence agriculture in the village with a world of towns, clerks, salaries, machines—the 'modern' world. Agriculture came to stand for backwardness and 'bush'; progress started with book-learning in the schools; and the young teachers and clerks with their better clothes and money salaries (however small) and their scraps of knowledge of a wider world confirmed this view. Nothing could have stopped Africans from seeking the towns and white collar work; nothing could have stopped the British workman early in this century from trying to get his child education and a white collar job out of the ruck, out of the dead-end labour of factory or mine. Indeed, just as some of the British workmen, who were the 'Africans' of Britain's nineteenth century, went to Working Men's Colleges, Ruskin's lectures, and later Tawney's classes, to learn about the stars and about foreign nations and socialism and philosophy, so the aspiring African wanted knowledge of the white man's world, and of the sources of his power and of political philosophies which could be used to gain a share of it; he did not want lectures on soil erosion or on manuring his *shamba*.

But if we must look much deeper than colonial stupidity for the causes of African attachment to a literary education and a white collar job, it is true that, in detail, the syllabus was often unintelligently British—too much British history and British botany, too much learning in the class room and too little doing in the field. The culmination of this course became, all too easily, a good pass in School Certificate and eventually a degree in Arts or in Science on the traditional lines of the British university. Certainly, as Evans points out, the idiom of teaching could have been far more rural and more African; certainly it seemed strange to see the books on Anglo-Saxon in African university colleges, through which the London English syllabus had to be approached. Indeed, it can seem intolerably perverse, at least at first impression, that such studies should be solemnly proceeding in an African society faced by urgent and strongly felt shortages of men to take over the practical jobs of running their own society.

In a word, the British tradition of education probably brought Africans more quickly than any other could have done into the company of the Western-educated world. It gave them the new horizons, for which they longed, and it gave them the qualifications for direct entry into Western institutions, to their great benefit. But it took them very little of the way to their next task—that of running the machinery of their own society and, especially, of reforming radically their own agricultural custom and techniques. The reaction from African governments against this situation raises one of the policy issues for later discussion.

4. LEGACIES—CONDITIONS, EQUIPMENT, STAFF

It is easy to forget, in talking of universities and technical colleges, that East African societies are still poor—an income per head of around £20 (Uganda and Tanganyika) or £30 (Kenya)—and were much poorer. Not only were primary schools the simplest of buildings —some thatched classrooms, an open-sided 'hall' with wooden benches for assembly, an open piece of grass for a playground. Secondary schools were—and many still are—based on simple African standards. The dormitories, long barns with the simplest bedsteads two feet apart; the classrooms, rows of desks facing a blackboard; the dining room, often an open-sided barn with benches and wooden trestles; the kitchen, a smoke-blackened corner with vast iron pots on wood-burning stoves; the food, maize porridge, vegetables, relishes, a little meat (the normal financial allowance for food would be about 11d to 1s 3d per boy per day); the light, an electric plant on the site, often turned off by 9.0 p.m.; the laboratory just adequate, with sinks and 'Afrigas', but rarely, until recently, with electric power; the library a meagre collection of books, not always in a room of its own. These conditions until very recently applied also to many training centres for agricultural staff, for teachers, for apprentices in the trade schools.

Within this simple style and low cost some of the older and best secondary schools achieved an extremely pleasant rurally civilized atmosphere. Their white-washed buildings lie well scattered among shade trees, with acres of cut grass between them; flowering trees and shrubs, well kept playing fields, often a central quadrangle of classrooms with some shape and dignity, pleasant staff houses and gardens make up a good environment, and in a sunny climate. But in the last six or seven years, and particularly in the last three, some (but not all) secondary schools have begun to adopt far higher standards. Instead of General Science, the school takes physics with chemistry or even physics and chemistry separately—a new laboratory is needed. Some schools move on to a Sixth Form— and their Sixth Formers will be young men or girls of twenty to twenty-three; they need far more books, a proper library and reading room, perhaps even some privacy for quiet study. So, here and there, on an increasing scale, new buildings, architect designed, are going up on the old sites; more mains electricity is available; film projectors and tape-recorders make their appearance; old buildings are refurbished, adapted; Trusts, Foundations, CD & W, American aid provide a theatre, a fine assembly hall or chapel. In consequence, the schools are at present a strange mixture of ancient and modern, and this applies to many training centres too. Maintenance grants have not kept pace with the new buildings; in most cases 1s a day is still the food allowance, and the wooden benches are still good enough to last a few more years.

This transitional stage at secondary level would have no special significance but for comparison—above all with the university colleges. For once a boy can enter the Royal College in Nairobi, he enters another world—a very superior world indeed. The latest modern architecture in five or six storeys surround him; concealed lighting, a vast library, European food (it is now 10s per head), adult clothes in place of his schoolboy shirt and shorts, a hostel (also modern), freedom, Nairobi at his feet, learned Professors to give lectures—this is a staggering difference from his school up-country with its kindly authoritarian Headmaster, the maize meal, the flickering electric light, and the school rules. The gap which has opened between the university level of provision and the level of secondary schools and training centres, enhancing the already over-rated prestige of a Degree, disquieting the schools, swallowing up revenue, is in itself an element in the educational policy problems which have to be discussed.

Finally, there is the question of staff. African secondary schools in East Africa with 100 per cent trained teachers, with a high percentage of graduates, are still far ahead of most West African countries—because the teachers are still largely expatriates. The same applies largely to the agricultural, medical, police and other governmental training centres, where the staff are mainly drawn from trained field officers. Only in the primary schools and in the trade schools and technical institutes is the standard far lower than is now necessary. Primary schools ought to have for their top four

Standards African teachers with a School Certificate pass and two years subsequent training in a college. These teachers are paid about £320 per annum—a salary wholly unattractive to a boy with School Certificate for whom, as will appear, so many more attractive and lucrative openings are available. The trade schools, training artisans, attracted mainly teachers of the type of a competent Naval Petty Officer (old style), thoroughly efficient in his technical know-how, often wholly untrained in teaching methods, sometimes very shaky on the science underlying the job he well knows how to do. Some staff of this type moved on into the higher level of the technical colleges; and there is little doubt that, up to 1961, the whole standard of technical training in most institutions reflected the old, colonial, empirical, handyman tradition rather than modern standards of technical education. Here again, policy issues will arise.

5. GROWTH TO THE MID-1950S.

A detailed account of the phases and controversies in the growth of African education would not be relevant to this book. It is characterized in the early stages by a long effort, constantly met by disappointments, to get children into school at all, and to keep them there long enough to make any lasting impression: the vast majority left after from two to four years in primary school. The second phase swings to the opposite extreme—a desperate effort to provide enough schools for the mobs of children eager to come, and to provide places in intermediate and secondary education for the swelling numbers who wished to stay on.

By the mid-1950s, the stage reached can be roughly described as follows. First, in the central school stream the primary and secondary system was well established. Table 1 (see over) shows the number of African School Certificate passes for the three countries year by year. Moreover, there was a growing provision for higher education. Makerere College in Uganda started in 1948 to provide a two-year pre-university course for the whole of East Africa with School Certificate entry; and in 1950 the College took the first entrants from this course into a degree course under the regulations of London University. The educational pyramid was still exceedingly narrow at the top. Figures for 1957 in Kenya show that about 80 per cent of boys and 32 per cent of girls of school age found a place in school; but the figures of their distribution tell their own tale:

Kenya African[1] Schools		Enrolment 1957			SC Passes		
		Boys	Girls	Total	Boys	Girls	Total
3,414	Primary	315,807	125,111	440,918			
474	Intermediate	47,646	11,702	59,348			
25	Secondary	2,798	336	3,134	341	22	363

[1] Source: Kenya Education Dept., *Triennial Survey 1955–1957*.

In the same year 69 Kenyan boys entered Makerere and 57 were enrolled at the Royal Technical College, Nairobi. It is as well to remember that this state of affairs existed only six years ago.

African Passes in Cambridge Overseas School Certificate

	KENYA			UGANDA			TANGANYIKA
	Boys	*Girls*	*Total*	*Boys*	*Girls*	*Total*	*Total*
1940	7 (11)	—	7	5 (7)	—	5	—
1941	* (16)	—	*	10 (20)	—	10	—
1942	11 (16)	—	11	8 (13)	—	8	—
1943	13 (15)	—	13	18 (24)	—	18	—
1944	11 (11)	—	11	19 (20)	—	19	—
1945	17	—	17	18 (24)	—	18	—
1946	38	—	38	16 (29)	2 (3)	18	—
1947	35	—	35	55	—	55	4 (5)
1948	38	—	38	84	—	84	15 (28)
1949	60 (61)	—	60	104	4	108	30 (42)
1950	63 (65)	—	63	96 (135)	? (7)	96+	34 (43)
1951	87 (87)	1 (1)	88	135 (204)	9 (13)	144	57 (67)
1952	99 (106)	2 (2)	101	187 (324)	5 (9)	192	64 (87)
1953	139 (148)	5 (5)	144	192 (292)	6 (7)	198	86 (103)
1954	153 (165)	9 (10)	162	206 (245)	21 (25)	227	98 (105)
1955	226 (245)	7 (7)	233	276 (355)	20 (28)	296	118 (131)
1956	283 (368)	16 (16)	299	333 (478)	23 (39)	356	139 (145)
1957	341 (361)	22 (22)	363	456 (615)	35 (50)	491	149 (150)
1958	451 (584)	40 (41)	491	525 (679)	32 (37)	557	170 (175)
1959	605 (746)	49 (53)	654	545 (678)	49 (65)	594	293 (324)
1960	580 (900)	69 (85)	649	703 (775)	68 (76)	771	460 (478)
1961	860 (1,372)	91 (110)	951	592	68	660	439 (573)
Total			4,428			4,925	2,156

Note: Figures in brackets indicate number of candidates.
   * Scripts lost by enemy action.

It is worth listing the principal training opportunities which were available around this time to boys and girls at the level of Standard VIII and of School Certificate (Form 4 secondary). There is a slight overlap because at that time many pupils left school at Form 2 (Standard X in Tanganyika) and, simultaneously, the training institutions with Standard VIII entry were trying to attract Form 2 leavers, while those with Form 4 entry had to make do with some from Form 2.

Training Opportunities for Boys post-Standard VIII—Kenya 1957[1]

Teacher training	(2 years to become lower primary school teachers)
Trade and technical schools	(3 or 4 years. About 1,000 places in 5 schools)
East African Railways and Harbours	(5 year apprenticeship—all 3 territories)
Kenya Police	(600–700 places—6-month course for Constables)
Medical Training Centre	(2- to 4-year courses—Hospital Assistants; Graded Dressers, Health Assistants; Assistant Midwives; Assistant Health Visitors; Darkroom and Entomological Assistants, etc.—about 500 in all under training)
Agricultural training	(2 colleges, 2-year course for Agricultural and Veterinary Assistants)
Commercial and Industrial	(6 or 8 largest firms with regular training schemes)

Training Opportunities for Boys with School Certificate—Kenya 1957[2]

Teacher training	(2 years to become intermediate or junior secondary teachers)
Royal Technical College	(3-year courses—250 places. Architecture (Intermediate Exam., RIBA), Engineering (to Common Part I of Institutes of Civil, Mechanical and Electrical Engineers), Commerce, Survey, Science (leading to GCE(A))

[1] Source: G. & L. Hunter, *Report to Beit and Dulverton Trustees* (Colleges of Citizenship), 1958.
[2] *Ibid.*

Kabete Technical and Trade School	(20/25 places, 15-month course in Commercial and Clerical training)
East African Railways & Harbours	(About 10 per cent of intake at SC level)
Kenya Police	(3-month training for Inspectors)
E. A. Posts and Telecommunications	(Up to 2-year courses. 350/400 places)
E. A. School of Co-operation	(6 to 7-month course)
Medical Training Centre	(3- or 4-year courses—Assistant Health Inspectors, Assistant Radiographers, Dispensers, Laboratory Assistants, Orthopaedic Assistants. About 100 in all under training)
Agricultural Training	(Small proportion of intake by now Form 2 and Form 4).

These lists cover only the most important divisions, where a formal training was available. There were of course many other opportunities for employment for Africans, particularly in clerical grades; and some other government departments offered training, notably the Ministry of Works, the Forestry and Game Departments, the Water Department and various branches of the East Africa High Commission.

Some special features of these lists should be noted. First, teacher training represented the largest single intake. Each country, with over 10,000 teachers, was offering annually 700 or 800 places at various levels. Second, opportunities for girls were still limited virtually to teaching, nursing and domestic science (for which a good course was opened at the Royal Technical College). A very few managed to gain employment as 'demonstrators' for Singer Sewing Machines, and some obtained training in Community Development; commercial training, including stenography, was still almost entirely lacking for African girls.

Third, the variety of training for government work, particularly in agriculture, the medical department, co-operation, police and of course education, is worth some attention. It became the practice in all three countries for the government to establish quite large training centres, under departmental control; and these are an important feature of the educational planning of the 1960s and will be discussed later.

On the technical side, the emergence of the Royal Technical College in Nairobi (to be matched by the Kampala Technical

Institute and a similar Institute in Dar-es-Salaam) is of some significance. It had been recognized that the trade schools in Kenya and Tanganyika and the technical schools, of which no less than twelve were established in Uganda, were not adequate for the more modern training to higher levels which was becoming necessary with the growth of industry and commerce. Most of them did not even attempt City and Guilds qualifications; and they concentrated mainly on the building and allied trades—carpenters, masons, painters; electrical and proper engineering trades were poorly represented and seldom carried to a high level of competence. Unfortunately, none of the three technical institutes had a good start. The Nairobi Royal Technical College, which drew a substantial endowment from the Gandhi Memorial Trust, was haunted by a certain obligation to the Trust to provide higher education in the Arts and by an ambition to become a university. In consequence it never settled to the practical, humdrum but vitally necessary task of a straightforward technical college. It was fortunate when the college achieved its ambition, becoming the Royal College and part of the University of East Africa, and the Kenya Polytechnic was created to give the necessary technical and commercial courses. In Uganda and Tanganyika, for different reasons, the colleges did not at first thrive, and both were to be reorganised and revitalised in 1961/2.

Finally, there was a sprinkling of Africans at higher levels. Some were coming out from Makerere with Degrees or diplomas, some returning from overseas universities to which they obtained grants or scholarships, partly through the Missions, partly through American offers, partly through grants and scholarships given by the British Council and partly through the territorial governments. Yet it was noticeable in 1957 that there was little sense of urgency in the government policies. The idea of rapid Africanisation of the Civil Services was barely born, although some preliminary planning had gone on, notably in Uganda. Dr Nyerere had only just appeared powerfully on the scene; the first Lancaster House conference for Kenya was still two years ahead; Independence for Uganda was not yet on the agenda. There were perhaps a dozen African graduates in administrative levels in the Kenya Civil Service, some lawyers and senior men in the Kabaka's government in Uganda, an even tinier group of graduates or professionals in Tanganyika, which at that time was lagging behind the other two territories both in education and in income per head. Yet although these African graduates were few in number, their influence was great in at least one respect. They spread far and wide among Africans the prestige of a university Degree and the then even greater prestige of an overseas education. It was in the period between the end of the

War and about 1960 that the pressure to go abroad built up to its highest peak.

6. THE NEW URGENCY—1957–1963

It was from about 1957 that a new educational tempo began to be felt, accelerating slowly up to 1959 and thereafter with extreme speed. It was felt perhaps first in Kenya in about 1956 when the end of the Mau Mau Emergency stimulated the whole European community and the Government in particular to accelerate the training of Africans to occupy responsible positions. Training was increased and improved particularly for the African staff of African District Councils and in agriculture. Firms began to think seriously of taking in African management trainees; ideas of a multi-racial society were in the wind; to the lasting credit of the Kenya European community a far more positive attitude towards African advancement was the outcome of an experience which might well have led to revengeful repression. The Swynnerton Plan for Kenya agriculture implied more extensive training for Africans and created, in one sphere at least, an atmosphere of purposeful advance. The Education Department, under mounting pressure for more school places, embarked on a major programme both at intermediate and at secondary level—the number of secondary schools in Kenya rose from eighteen in 1955 to fifty in 1961. Tanganyika was next to feel the wind as TANU swept towards power; Uganda was last.

It is from this period that there starts, on all sides, a keen competition to attract and employ Africans with a School Certificate pass. The Agriculture and Medical Departments saw the opportunity to raise entry standards and produce a higher grade of staff; large companies, the Railways, Posts and Telegraphs, the technical colleges, Makerere, Mr Mboya with his Airlift, American universities, the Police and Armed Services were soon all in the race; lagging behind, owing to salary difficulties, but needing men more urgently than any, came the Education Departments, in search of teachers for their swelling school programmes. Simultaneously, from 1958 onwards in Kenya and a little later elsewhere, the market for the Standard VIII school leaver began to drop, partly because the output was increasing so fast, partly because entry qualifications to training and employment were being raised. The boy with only primary education was starting his long journey downwards into the general level of the population, save for those who could train as teachers; from then on the trade schools could tell a dismal story of 5,000 applications for 50 vacancies from boys of Standard VIII.

The last phase is current history—the sudden approach of independence, crash programmes for 'Africanisation', emergency expansion of secondary schools, the up-grading of the Royal Technical College to university college status, the foundation of another university college in Dar-es-Salaam, the foundation of the Kenya Institute of Administration and the Tanganyika centre at Mzumbe to train Africans for the provincial and central administration, the development of Sixth Forms in schools in order to accelerate the intake to the university, massive American aid, the appearance of the Iron Curtain countries, Western Europe, Ethiopia, Egypt, Israel, India and Peking in the lists of scholarship-givers, frantic efforts by government departments by in-service training and overseas secondments to maintain the required rate of Africanisation—all this and more makes up the emergency atmosphere in relation to all forms of education and training which pervades East Africa today. This is the scene which must be more closely analysed in the main body of this Study.

CHAPTER II

ASIAN AND EUROPEAN EDUCATION

Little need be said in this study about European education. In Uganda it has always been confined to primary education for the children of European civil servants and business men, who have used Kenyan secondary schools. In Tanganyika there has been one major mixed secondary school—St. Michael & St. George at Iringa —and a girls' primary school at Mbeya, now changing to an African school. The Tanganyika government decided in 1962 to close St Michael & St George—a residential public school with first-rate equipment and buildings—at the end of 1963, although Africans had been admitted and successfully 'integrated'. The reason appears to have been that the school, with a high staffing ratio and European-type food and facilities, would be too expensive, or if maintained for Africans would produce a privileged élite. The future of the buildings and staff was uncertain at the time of writing.

The secondary schools in Kenya have an uncertain future. The Prince of Wales, Duke of York and the girls' Kenya High School all have Sixth Forms and there are some other well-known schools— at Eldoret, Limuru, Mombasa and the Delamere High School in Nairobi. The Hospital Hill school (primary) in Nairobi has been multi-racial for some years. Africans, in small numbers, have been admitted to all these schools in the last three years, though they have not been able to pay the relatively high fees. The future obviously depends upon the future of the Kenya European farmers. It is fairly certain that only a very limited number of European boys and girls will enter the Kenya economy directly from any of these schools. The usual pattern was, in any case, for the secondary school leavers to go to universities in Britain (or South Africa), since Makerere, although open to all races, never attracted more than a handful of European students. For those Europeans who continue to take secondary schooling in Kenya, this pattern is likely to persist; and if they later come back to work in Kenya it will almost be on the same footing as 'expatriates', even though some Europeans may adopt Kenyan citizenship.

Europeans have, however, taken various forms of technical training in Kenya, both in the Royal Technical College (or now in the Polytechnic) and in some major in-service training schemes, such as that of East African Railways & Harbours. This technical training represented one of the few spheres in which young Europeans, Asians and Africans were likely to find themselves in a common class.

Asian education is in many ways more important for this study. Although in all three countries there is danger of considerable discrimination against Asians, particularly in access to important types of employment (notably, the public service), there is, at least at the time of writing, no visible reason to expect either a massive exodus of the Asian community or a serious breakdown of their educational system; but both could take place if African policy changes.

The biggest strain on this system is at present in Tanganyika, where all schools are now open to all races (though it is possible that entry will be restricted to Tanganyika citizens), with competitive entry into secondary schools. In general, a very high proportion of Asians have gone on to secondary education (it is compulsory in Kenya in Nairobi, Kisumu and Mombasa until fifteen), and without serious competition. Faced, in Tanganyika, by competition from an African population of 9,000,000, the Asian community of 120,000 can clearly foresee that, if competition is in fact quite unrestricted, and if no 'secondary modern' schools come into existence, a high proportion—indeed the vast majority—of Asian children will get no education, within the public system, after the age of twelve. In this they are, of course, in the same position as the Africans, of whom less than 10 per cent will enter secondary schools when the really large numbers are completing primary, although the Africans will probably be a year or two older, even if the primary course is reduced to seven years instead of eight.

The Asian community will feel this situation acutely. Far more of their schools were provided by the community, although grant-aided by government. Already very humble members of the community are contributing heavily to maintain their educational effort; but a complete maintenance of their school system would be beyond the power of the community, even with the usual generous help from the Aga Khan's Ismaili group. Moreover, the Asian approach to education is different, in subtle ways, from the African. The Harper-Woodhead Report[1] noted in 1957/8 in Kenya that Asians considered boys too young at fifteen to enter adult employment, and they were often kept at home between fifteen and seventeen. Family education plays a far bigger part and Asians have established a mixture of school (mainly day school) and home up to at least fifteen as the only

[1] *Report on Asian and European Education in Kenya, 1958*. Kenya Government Printer, Nairobi.

natural and proper way to bring up their sons and daughters. Although Asians have been no less anxious to pass examinations, and have had a teaching method even more mechanically instructional than the European-taught African secondary schools, they have perhaps cared not merely for the examination as a qualification for a job or for entry into higher education but as a sign that a child has acquired the knowledge which he or she should acquire. This attitude is evidenced by the insistence of the Asian community (against the strongest European opposition) that a child should not be promoted through the standards each year but should repeat, sometimes even three or four times, any standard until the necessary test for promotion has been successfully passed.

The effect of mechanical whole-class instruction in Asian schools, of the sometimes poor standard of English among the teachers, and of far less competitive entry into secondary school has been a much lower percentage of passes to entrants in the School Certificate examinations. The Harper-Woodhead Report calculated in 1958 that, of the European and Asian age-group eligible for secondary education between 1953/4 (Form 1) and 1957 (Form 4), 79 per cent of Europeans eligible were admitted in 1954, of whom 83 per cent gained School Certificate—i.e. 65.6 per cent of the age group. 42.6 per cent of Asians eligible were admitted, of whom 38 per cent passed School Certificate—i.e. 16.2 per cent of the age group. By 1961 in Kenya, 73.7 per cent of African entrants (boys) passed School Certificate, 82.3 per cent of European boys, but only 42.1 per cent of Asian boys.[1] It is fair to add that the Kenya Asians have constantly complained of poor buildings and equipment in their schools, and that Asian schools are virtually all *day* schools. Thus Asians, competing on the one hand with the 10 per cent cream of an African population from 30 times to 90 times their size in the 3 countries, and on the other hand with Europeans learning from the start in their own language in more lavish and better staffed schools, have not unnaturally come out badly. Their future prospects of secondary education are at present a cause of deep anxiety to them, and with good reason.

As to post-school training and employment, the Asians in the past have fared (and contributed) reasonably well. They have filled, in East Africa, certain clear-cut niches in the economy—as clerks, as artisans or technicians, as doctors, dentists and lawyers; as engineers, as building contractors, as plantation entrepreneurs (primarily in Uganda); as industrialists and processers (ginning, milling, biscuit factories, etc.), and in a wide range of commercial activities, from the large importer and wholesaler to the smallest retailer in the 'bush'.

---

[1] European girls, 94.5 per cent; African girls, 84.8 per cent; Asian girls 39.1 per cent.

At the lowest end of the scale there has always been great poverty—the owner of the village *duka*, with a pack of children, has lived on next to nothing. At the upper end there are a few very rich men. But throughout East Africa, and apart from the smallest retailer, the Asian occupies a middle place, between European and African. He is found as the supervisor of African artisans, the booking clerk, hairdresser, chemist, cashier-accountant, garage foreman (and owner), in the middle grades of the Civil Service, in catering, and above all as shopkeeper.

Asians have been eager to take what technical training they could find; but above all their skills have been passed on within the family—the Sikh teaches his son carpentry, the Gujarati trains his son and daughter to work in the shop; trade and business become second nature to families who live by it—and that is not to say that it is not learned. To abstract the Asian community from East Africa would be to cause immense economic damage, in ways not often considered, particularly in the whole distributive mechanism, in every form of maintenance—telephone, electric power, railways, lifts, motor vehicles, factory plant—and in the whole accounting and filing systems of the banks, the public service and industry.

In their relationship to Africans and Europeans, the Asian community fared badly. Europeans in East Africa have too often been, in this respect, unbearably arrogant. Like the landed aristocracy of England, they had far more sympathy with the peasant than with the clerk. The officials saw their task to lie in African advancement, often accusing the Asian of commercial exploitation. The farmers were concerned with their African staff. While all Europeans were cheerfully trying to turn Africans into Englishmen as fast as possible, they neither attempted to change nor really warmed to Asian ways of life, strongly entrenched in an old and most un-English culture. Naturally, there were individual exceptions and multi-racial groups. But it has only been in the last two or three years, when many Europeans began to find a fellow feeling with Asians as partners in political adversity, that the general European attitude has been more sympathetic.

Vis-à-vis the African population, the Asians occupied a peculiar position. On the one side they understood Africans better in some ways, spoke their language, employed them in face-to-face relationships, understood and even shared their poverty. Relations were much more intimate and, in a sense, real. But many adverse elements were there. Africans felt that Asian shopkeepers exploited them—though the violent competition between six Asian shops in a single small centre, all selling the same goods, must have kept this within narrow bounds. Asians were accused, perhaps with more reason, of refusing to teach Africans their skills. Compared to the

European, the Asian had little magic or prestige in African eyes. Occupying the middle grades, the Asians seemed always to be the first obstacle to an African seeking advancement. As African political power has suddenly grown, the Asians have done their best to come to terms with it, by political support and by paying heavily in subscriptions and donations to causes favoured by the Africans. But their position is a perilous one; and most of them have no real line of retreat to India or Pakistan, where their living standards would fall in any case.

The great hope of the Asian community must lie in a rapid expansion of the East African economies, so that employment expands and there is room for Asian skills without causing too great African jealousy. Their second hope—and one which will be difficult to fulfil—is to keep a step ahead of the African in acquiring superior skills. But they see already, and they foresee more frighteningly in the future, a concentration of money and effort on African training and education which is already bringing a stream of Africans, soon to become a flood, into just the occupations (except for commercial enterprise) where the Asian advantage lay—in technical and clerical skills, in the professions and in the public service. In consequence, Asians are even more anxious to acquire a professional skill which is internationally accepted. For if there is no room for them in East Africa, there may well be room for doctors, scientists, nurses, even teachers in the affluent societies, whose public health services already contain many Asians and West Indians. The USA is a net *importer* of 'high level manpower' from the developing countries and Great Britain may well be the same, and they offer a high standard of living. At the present moment many young Asian students of medicine or law or engineering in Britain are likely to seek work here rather than in East Africa, and to acquire qualifications and experience which will give them a wider choice of home in a few years' time.

Thus it may well be that the Asian need for education overseas may become, in some senses, more desperate than the African; for Africans will have both a better share of what is available at home and far more offers of scholarships abroad. In the long run, it is to be hoped that all who can get and accept East African citizenship will have equal opportunity, without distinction of colour or culture or religion; this is certainly the aim Dr Nyerere has proclaimed, and with personal conviction. Whether he will succeed in establishing this policy in Tanganyika, whether Kenya and Uganda under African governments will adopt or execute it remains to be seen. In any case, Asians in East Africa will have to face some harsh realities. They are no longer in any degree a privileged group—and their easy entrance to secondary education was, in effect, a privilege over Africans. They will soon lose much of their technical and educational lead; they will have to accept the position of a small minority community, without any special collective rights, competing with a huge majority of newly enfranchised Africans for their share—at most—of educational and employment opportunity. The manpower estimates which follow in chapters IV and V show how large a part this minority plays at present in services vital to the future prosperity of Kenya. It will not be in the interests of African governments or peoples to destroy their contribution out of jealousy; but it will need wisdom on both sides, and particularly a full acceptance of the new political power by Asians, if hardship and serious economic waste are to be avoided.

CHAPTER III

THE PRESENT FACTS

This chapter is designed simply to record a rather large mass of facts about the provision for education and training in East Africa, with comment which is mainly descriptive rather than critical. Sheer numbers have not much meaning save in relation to the demand for training and to the quality of institutions in which students are enrolled, and this qualitative assessment is dealt with in later chapters. But it is perhaps better to record the facts at this early point, so that they can form a point of reference. The relevance of numbers to 'manpower' requirements will be discussed in chapter V. Where it is possible, the figures are given by race; but this will become increasingly difficult in future, owing to the integration of schools, which is happening to some degree in Kenya and Uganda and is formally established in Tanganyika, so that separate statistics will not be given there any more. This is another reason why it may be useful to record the main facts in one place, before the racial element is obscured in the figures published by local governments. The reader not interested in schools figures could well move on to Section 1 (d) of this chapter.

I. THE SCHOOLS[1]

(a) *Enrolments and Examination Passes*

KENYA, *1961*

		Primary		Secondary	
		(a)I–IV	*(b)V–VIII*	*(a) 1–4*	*(b) 5–6*
Africans	*Boys*	435,000	121,850	5,200	166
	Girls	220,850	34,050	1,050	—
	Total	655,850	155,900	6,250	166

	Primary	Secondary
Asians	44,477[2]	12,676[2]
Europeans	8,233	3,507

[1] The figures in the following section on schools are derived from a number of sources—Reports of the Education Depts., especially obtained figures, World Bank Reports, Africanisation Reports, Development Plan Reports, Papers for the Princeton Conference 1960 and the Oxford Conference on Tensions in Development, 1961. These have been put together so that a single Table may rely on 4 sources; I felt it unnecessary and confusing to add references to each figure.

[2] Includes Arabs and Goans (7,090 primary and 1,595 secondary).

Kenya African Preliminary Examination Candidates 1961   22,183 (12,326 passed)
School Certificate Passes, 1961

	African	860 of which 9 girls
	Asian	901 of which 325 girls
	European	480 of which 242 girls

Note:

Africans enrolled in Standard I	in 1961 were	182,227 (68,407 girls)
Standard IV		163,096 (47,244)
Standard V		67,488 (17,247)
Standard VIII		22,485 (3,982)
Form 1		2,194 (464)
Form 4		1,054 (103)

These enrolments by class show two factors, not here distinguished, viz. the facts that the 22,000 in Standard VIII in 1961 represent both a smaller enrolment in Standard I eight years earlier and a very considerable 'fall out' between Standards IV and V four years earlier. But since they also show 67,500 pupils in Standard V in 1961, it is likely that there will be at least 60,000 in Standard VIII in 1964, requiring secondary school places in 1965. The number of places likely to be available is estimated at about 4,000 in 1964 and might conceivably be 5,000 in 1965—i.e. less than 10 per cent of the probable candidates. Thereafter, the numbers of candidates for secondary school places is likely to rise extremely steeply to a figure around 150,000 in 1968. It is clear that no conceivable expansion of secondary education is likely to be able to offer 15,000 secondary places by that time. Although the proportion of the *age group* receiving secondary education will be rising fast, the proportion of primary school leavers entering secondary school may drop to 5 per cent or 6 per cent at that point. Thus for the next seven or eight years at least the competitive pressure to get entry into secondary schools will be immense, and increasing.

UGANDA, 1961

	Primary	*Junior Secondary*	*Secondary*
Africans	370,436	21,881	4,434
Asians	15,635	3,633	2,591
Europeans	1,224	—	—

African School Certificate Passes, 1961 were 732
Asian School Certificate Passes, 1960   194

Note: By 1962 the numbers leaving junior secondary schools were approximately 12,000 per year, and the entry into secondary was nearly 2,000 Africans. The main fall out in Uganda takes place between the end of primary (Standard VI) and entry into junior secondary (seventh year); in 1960 the enrolment in Standard VI was 35,307, of whom not more than 10,000 can have entered junior secondary schools in 1961. By 1964 the numbers completing primary Standard VI are estimated to reach about 55,000, and the World Bank Mission felt that if half entered junior secondary, i.e. 28,000, it would be reasonable. It will be fairly easily possible to provide an entry of between 3,500 and 4,000 to secondary schools by 1965, thus giving places to about 12½ per cent–13 per cent of those who complete eight years, but to only 6½ per cent of those completing six years of primary education. Thus the pressure for secondary school places will be equally high in Uganda.

TANGANYIKA, NOVEMBER 1961

	Primary	*Secondary*
Africans I—IV	450,644	
V—VIII	55,616	
Total	506,260	6,031
Asians, Goans, Others	17,297	9,991
Europeans	1,883	679

The significant breaks in the figures (breaks almost entirely due to African wastage) are, in 1961:

	African	*Asian*	*European*
Standard I	138,570	3,000	400
IV	93,978	2,900	350
V	18,465	2,800	200
VIII	9,715	2,045	150
Form 1 entry	2,163	1,914	119
4	687	700	60

Obviously, while the Asian numbers run consistently along, dropping only by about 1,000 from Standard I to Standard VIII, and suffer their worst drop (they are more than halved) between Form 2 and Form 3, the African figures are reduced at one blow from 94,000 in Standard IV to 18,500 at Standard V; entry into secondary from Standard VIII (9,700) to Form 1 (2,163) gives over 25 per cent of secondary places for those who reach Standard VIII. But there is another severe loss after Form 2, reducing numbers from 1,800 to around 1,100. This loss at Form 2 is being remedied very quickly: it is estimated that by 1965 over 2,000 Africans will be taking School Certificate in Form 4, against the 540 in 1961.

School Certificate Passes, 1961
African	407 boys & (?) 32 girls
Asian	560 (?400 boys, 160 girls).

(b) A Note on Sixth Forms

The Higher School Certificate course in African schools in East Africa was first started in four Tanganyika schools (Tabora Government Secondary, St Francis, Pugu, St Andrew's, Minaki, and Tabora Girls' School) in 1959. By 1962, excluding European schools, 11 schools in Kenya, 8 in Tanganyika and 12 in Uganda were running this course. Africans were also being admitted, though in small numbers, to some previously European schools, including the Duke of York, Prince of Wales and Kenya High School for Girls in Kenya, and to St Michael & St George School in Tanganyika. (Before the HSC course was opened in schools a 2-year pre-entry course was run centrally for East Africa at Makerere.)

Entry to the HSC examination in 1962:

	Candidates	Passes
Kenya	353	161
Uganda	159	73
Tanganyika	205	106

Estimates for entries and passes for the 5-year period 1961–65 are given below. The development of Sixth Form work is a critical issue of policy, discussed in more detail in later chapters.[1]

(c) *Projections of Future Secondary Output*

The Education Departments of three Governments have made various estimates of the probable number of candidates taking and passing School Certificate—obviously the estimates up to 1965, which relate to the pupils already in Form 1 in 1962, are more reliable than the more distant targets.

Estimated Output Form 4—(a) 1961–65

	Total	SC Passes		Fail
Kenya	Entrants	Division I & II	Division III or GCE	
African	9,000	4,150	2,700	2,150
Asian	7,500	2,600	2,600	2,300
European	2,800	2,000	500	300
	19,300	8,750	5,800	4,750
Uganda[2]				
(Estimate)	9,000	6,500 (I, II III)	1,000 (GCE)	1,500
Tanganyika	15,000	7,000	3,000	5,000

Estimated Output Form 4—(b) 1966–71[3]

Kenya	Pass	Fail
African	16,000	8,000
Asian	8,000	4,000
European	2,000	1,000
	26,000	13,000
Uganda	11,500	3,000
Tanganyika	16,000	9,000

[1] The schools with Sixth Forms were as follows in 1962:

Tanganyika: Tabora (Boys); Tabora (Girls); St Francis, Pugu; St Andrew's, Minaki; Ihungu (Bukoba); Moshi, and two Asian schools (Dares-Salaam and Karimjee School, Tanga).

Kenya: Alliance High School; Shimo-la-Tewa (Coast); Kisii; Kakamega; Kamusinga; Kangaru (Embu); African Girls' High School (Kikuyu); Strathmore College (Nairobi), and three Asian schools (Duke of Gloucester (boys); Duchess of Gloucester (girls) and Kisumu).

Uganda: Budo; Busoga College; Gayaza (girls); Kisubi; Makerere College School; Nabbingo (girls); Namilyango; Ntare, and four primarily Asian schools to which Africans are admitted—Mbale, Kololo, Old Kampala and H.H. the Aga Khan school.

[2] The rough estimate is for about 1,500 African passes in 1965. Asian passes are assumed to rise very slowly to 300 in 1965 from 220 in 1961.

[3] Inevitably rough guesses, based on the proportion of SC passes likely to enter HSC courses or GCE(A) courses.

Estimated Output at HSC

Kenya	Total Entrants	(a) 1961–65 Pass	Fail	(b) 1966–71 Pass	Fail
African	1,000	550	450	2,400	1,100
Asian	600	370	230	600	400
European	500	415	85	?	?
	2,100	1,335	765	(3,000)	(1,500)
Uganda	1,560	960	600	2,600	1,300
Tanganyika	1,550	950	600	3,000	1,500

(d) *The Main Issues Revealed*

From these figures certain broad issues are revealed which are common to the three countries, though differing to some extent in time and scale. The numbers in each class reflect two main historical facts: first, the smaller intake eight years ago at Standard I, which is reflected in smaller numbers at Standard VIII today; and second, the heavy fall-out between Standards IV and V in Kenya and Tanganyika (or Standards VI and VII in Uganda), which further reduces the Standard VIII numbers. In secondary education there was, until recently, an examination at Form 2 and this, especially in Tanganyika, produces another drop between Forms 2 and 3. On these relatively low Standard VIII numbers it has been possible to take 10 per cent or even more on into secondary education.

But while the 1961/2 figures necessarily reflect events from 1953 onwards, the current situation is what matters for 1962/1970. And in the current situation, the large intakes at Standard I in the last three or four years are remorselessly working their way upwards, with a smaller fall-out at Standard IV, to produce relatively huge numbers completing primary from about 1964 onwards and demanding secondary school places. Even the rapid expansion of secondary schools, now in progress, cannot hope to give 10 per cent of primary leavers a place in Form 1 by 1964, and figures nearer 5 per cent or 6 per cent may be common from 1964 to 1968.

The second common conclusion is, in a sense, more encouraging. For the absolute numbers in secondary education are rising fast, and the projections for total numbers passing School Certificate or GCE in the decade 1961–1971 look very impressive in relation to the trickle available at that level in the early '50s. The following are estimated 5-year totals:

	1961–1966	1966–1971
Kenya	14,550	26,000 (24,000 without Europeans)
Uganda	7,500	11,500
Tanganyika	10,000	16,000

The Tanganyika figures are roughly in line with Uganda, allowing for the population proportion of 9 million to 6 million. Kenya is disproportionately ahead of both, partly through a larger secondary school programme and partly through a higher Asian population which is assumed to remain in Kenya. The Uganda figures may be on the low side; but Uganda has a higher proportion of Africans in the total figure. Manpower requirements in Uganda are, however, somewhat lower at present because the economy is sluggish, particularly in industrial development.

Finally, the relatively low estimates for passes in Higher School Certificate reflect the late development of Sixth Forms and the high standards of entry (Division I or the top 30 per cent of Division II School Certificate pass has normally been required). A considerably larger number of pupils will no doubt reach an Advanced Level pass in GCE by various means, even if they do not pass Higher School Certificate; and a proportion, impossible to estimate, will go overseas to colleges at School Certificate level in those countries or institutions which are prepared to offer scholarships at that point.

2. TECHNICAL EDUCATION AND INDUSTRIAL TRAINING

(a) *Rural Crafts*

The simplest level of 'technical' training, developed in some degree in all three countries, lies in small centres or clubs for training rural crafts, simple building, and domestic skills for women and girls. These were developed for obvious reasons, especially for boys and girls who left school early—often at Standard IV. In Kenya a special effort was made after Mau Mau to give something useful to do to boys in enforced idleness, and the practical training was often combined with some further schooling, sometimes to enable a boy to pass the Standard VIII examination externally. In Uganda a formal scheme of rural trade, homecraft and farm schools was established as a sequel to Standard VI primary; and in 1959 2,260 boys and 503 girls in their seventh, eighth or ninth years of education were enrolled in no less than 79 schools.[1] Rural training was also associated with the 12 'Development Centres' established for the general improvement of rural health, agriculture and social life. These Development Centres were reinforced by training courses at a central college (Nsamizi) which ran a wide variety of courses in aid of local administration, co-operatives and Community Development.

In Kenya the simplest level of craft work, largely of a hobby type, has been in over 150 youth clubs (a further 150 were planned

[1] Education Department Report, 1959.

in 1962)—a small number of boys from these clubs reach the level of the Labour Department's Trade Test and become full-time artisans.[1] There are also 12 rural training centres, run by voluntary agencies with some grant aid, a few of which reach virtually to trade school standards.

In Tanganyika the provision for rural craft training is not so formalized, although there have been a wide variety of small centres and courses connected with community development and agricultural training—one of the most successful courses for artisan training was at the prison in Dar-es-Salaam. The Kilimanjaro Native Co-operative Union (Chagga coffee growers) College at Moshi provides some domestic science and commercial courses on a more formal, but local, basis.

(b) *Trade Schools and Secondary Technical Schools*

These are government artisan-training centres, most highly developed in Kenya. The five established trade schools (Kabete, Thika, Nyanza, Coast, Machakos) had a total enrolment (March 31 1962) of 936, and the distribution of trades is of some interest:

Carpenters	267		Shoemakers	19
Builders	215		Tailors	44
Painters	72	621	Sheet Metal	24
Plumbers	67		B/S Welders	34
Electricians	39		Water charge-	
Fitters	15		hands	11
Turners	24		Pre-Secretarial	47
Mechanics	58			
			Total (all trades)	936

The fact that 621 out of 936 are trained for building and decorating (3 of the 5 schools have only these trades with, in one case, tailoring) requires some emphasis, since in fact there is a surplus, currently, partly owing to the building recession. Carpenters and some other less qualified boys are, of course, also coming out from the voluntary and rural centres mentioned above. The products of the trade schools take a Grade III Trade Test, and some are retained for a further year to take the Grade II test. The output in recent years has been: 1959—199 Grade III artisans; 1960—309 and 1961—649. The steep increase in 1961 is due to reduction in the length of course from 3 (or 4) years to 2 years; future output is likely to drop in 1962 to about 490 and rise again to about 550 when two new schools (Mawego in South Nyanza and Eldoret) come into full operation—Mawego is an up-graded rural training centre and

[1] I am much indebted for this and other information on technical training to Mr Nuttall, Technical Education Department, Nairobi.

Eldoret opened in January 1963. There is no doubt that a switch of emphasis away from the building trades towards electrical and mechanical work is overdue. Properly trained electricians, radio mechanics, engineering fitters could get a dozen jobs in Kenya, while unemployed masons and carpenters are walking the streets. Technical teacher training courses for the trade school staffs are now (somewhat belatedly) being vigorously pursued and all staff should be fully trained by 1965/6.

There have been four secondary technical schools in Kenya, providing a broadly based secondary education with a technical bias. One is attached to the Kabete Trade School, two are Asian schools in Nairobi and Mombasa, and the fourth is the Mombasa Institute of Muslim Education—the total annual output is between 100 and 125 boys, and this may be compared with a total of over 5,000 boys and girls leaving academic secondary schools in Kenya in 1962. Proposals are under consideration to add 6 more secondary technical schools, with an annual output of 80 each, so that there is a total output of 600 per annum by 1970.

In Tanganyika the two main trade schools, at Moshi and Ifunda, have followed a similar programme, though with rather less success. The Ifunda school, situated in the Southern Highlands far from any industry (it was originally a Polish refugee camp and subsequently a training centre for the Groundnut Scheme), had a first artisan output in 1953. Moshi opened in 1957. Unfortunately in 1959 a series of strikes broke out at both schools which resulted in practically the whole student population being expelled, and new classes were started in 1960. The total output from both schools up to 1961 was 872, of which over half were in building and decorating. The 1962 output still shows 214 in building and electrical wiring as against 145 in engineering trades. Trade Testing in Tanganyika has not been developed as effectively as in Kenya and Uganda. Proposals for a radical review of trade school policy have been made.[1]

In Uganda, development followed a slightly different pattern. Twelve secondary technical schools were established, widely scattered over a predominantly agricultural country. Their intake was at Standard VI (the end of Uganda primary) or occasionally at Standard VIII. In 1961 the enrolment was 1,100, although there were boarding places for 1,600 and some day pupils could have been taken as well. This experiment was not wholly successful, since the technical training did not reach clear standards, nor were the schools popular since they did not lead to any reasonably paid or progressive career. The World Bank Mission has proposed, and the Uganda

[1] G. Tobias, 'Survey of High-Level Manpower Requirements and Resources', Tanganyika Government, 1962. I am indebted to this survey for much useful information.

Government has accepted, that probably ten out of the twelve should be turned into 'senior' technical secondary schools (i.e. with entry to a Form 1 at the usual level for secondary grammar schools), following a craft or 'modern' syllabus to GCE(O) level and accommodating initially just over 2,000 pupils, as an addition to the main secondary programme of expansion. The remaining two technical schools, with 200 pupils each, would be wholly technical. The older form of the Kampala Technical Institute (it is being reorganized—see below) should also be mentioned here, as it operated partly as a trade school, though with an unacceptably heavy rate of failure to achieve full technical qualifications.

(c) *Technical Institutes and Colleges*

The next level of publicly-provided technical education consists of the technical institutes—the Kampala Technical Institute in Uganda; the Institute & Polytechnic in Nairobi and the Muslim Institute in Mombasa; the Dar-es-Salaam Technical Institute and the KNCU College of Commerce at Moshi, Tanganyika. All are well advanced in a process of transformation into modern technical colleges, with the Kenya Polytechnic (a new foundation taking over from the Royal Technical College) most advanced and the Kampala Technical Institute still in the throes of reorganization with the aid of massive assistance from UNESCO.

The Kenya Polytechnic and Technical Institute are housed in the same building in Nairobi and are virtually a unity. By September 1962 the Institute had enrolled about 600 students of all races (the proportion of all students in June 1962 at the Institute and Polytechnic was: Africans, 59.5 per cent; Asians, 33.7 per cent; Europeans, 6.8 per cent). These students are in employment and mainly attend one day plus one evening per week. They are being prepared for elementary and advanced examinations of the City & Guilds Institute in mechanical, civil and electrical engineering, building, telecommunications, some recognized commercial subjects and domestic science. In addition, the Polytechnic in June 1962 had 396 students engaged on courses of the level of Ordinary (National)[1] Certificate or higher, and this number reached over 500 by the winter of 1962. These courses include, as well as engineering, professional accountancy and GCE(A) courses, mainly in science subjects. It is interesting to note that 179 students were sent by the Government on 'localization' courses. The UN Special Fund, through UNESCO, was starting, in late 1962, to equip and staff further courses leading to Higher (National)[1] Certificate. The British Council for Technical Education & Training in Overseas

[1] The word 'National' is omitted overseas, since the level, though similar, is not the same.

Countries has approved a grant of £80,000 for a hostel to take 100 students in double study-bedrooms, to provide for students from the provinces.

With the 1,100–1,200 students enrolled by the winter of 1962, the present buildings will be used to capacity, without as yet fulfilling the demand from local industry for additional places and some new subjects. It is proposed when funds are available to build a 10- or 12-storey block on the site, at a cost of about £250,000 including equipment, to provide additional workshops, laboratories, classrooms, drawing offices and staff and student facilities. This would expand capacity by up to 600 students.

The Mombasa Institute is barely comparable with Nairobi—about 140 part-time evening students were enrolled in June 1962, far below the capacity of the buildings. There is no technical institute in Kisumu, or indeed elsewhere in Kenya. The main need at this level will be to provide at least good evening classes in the provinces, possibly backed by correspondence courses, to give an opportunity of technical or commercial education to boys and girls who cannot go to Nairobi.

The Technical Institute in Dar-es-Salaam started life in the nucleus of its present buildings in 1958—it had been preceded by a somewhat desultory provision of clerical classes which only grew from 19 students in 1950 to 34 seven years later in 1957. In 1958 in its new form it housed 75 full-time students, 157 on short intensive courses and 512 in evening classes; it was still providing a clerical and commercial syllabus. By 1962 the Institute had 245 students full-time, 341 on short intensive courses and 81 on part-time day courses, with 1,800 places in evening classes. The day-time courses were almost wholly pre-empted by the government for in-service or pre-service training—13 out of 18 courses were of this type and two of the remainder were filled by public services—Railways, Police, and Posts & Telecommunications. The evening classes covered English, book-keeping, typewriting, shorthand, GCE courses in English, physics, chemistry, mathematics, geography and economic history, as well as City & Guilds courses in building, motor mechanics, mechanical engineering and radio service.

The Institute is well equipped with buildings and workshops, at a cost of over £300,000, and has a formidable list of new requirements for approval and financing. It has a considerable library, mainly a gift from the Ford Foundation, and a hostel—further hostels for 50 girls and 120 boys are part of the additional requirements. Its main problem and weakness is the high proportion of government work and of commercial work, so that very little is being done for solid technician training for industry and commerce.

Full-time technical courses of the City & Guilds type will not be in production until 1964, and only about sixty students are at present scheduled for the secondary technical course.

The second unit in Tanganyika is the KNCU College at Moshi, which has mainly been giving two-year courses, with Standard X (Form 2) entry, in English, book-keeping, commerce, arithmetic, stenography, commercial law and geography. It is understood that the Co-operative Union may be willing to make the College over to the Tanganyika government, partly because recurrent expenditure has been high and partly because students have mainly moved into private rather than co-operative employment as was hoped. If this transfer took place, the combination of the KNCU College and Moshi Trade School would result in a second technical institute with commercial and engineering branches; this would also serve Arusha, fifty odd miles away, which may develop industrially, particularly if the Michelin Tyre factory is eventually established there.

Finally, in Uganda the Kampala Technical Institute has grown from three sources—the old Kampala Technical School (which was in effect a trade school), the Muljibhai Madhvani School of Commerce, and the Public Works Department engineering school, which at one time trained technical assistants for the PWD in the whole of East Africa. The buildings are on a good site at Kyambogo next to the main government teacher training college, with plenty of room for expansion. It has recently acquired a new library and will have an assembly hall in 1963, both through UK aid. The dormitory accommodation is, however, at present sub-standard and food allowance at the 1s 6d per day level.

The College at present includes the School of Building, the Muljibhai Madhvani School of Commerce, the School of Mechanical and Electrical Engineering, School of Science and Mathematics, Industrial Art and Women's Studies sections. It includes both GCE (O) and GCE(A) level courses. In the main, entry is at Form 4 (School Certificate) level, and in the Engineering School students can reach Ordinary (National) Certificate and may later proceed to the Higher Certificate. There is a close relation with Loughborough, to which students may go on to complete a Diploma of Technology.

The College is now being aided, to the extent of about £500,000, by UNESCO, mainly in the form of a dozen UNESCO staff, who will be attached to the College over the next few years for varying periods. The existing staff consists of 37 expatriates and 8 Africans, and the existing enrolment is running at about 400 full-time resident students—below the capacity of around 500. Expansion to about 1,000 resident students by 1967 is envisaged.

D

Two points of special interest were mentioned at this College. First, that the cost per student is about £585[1] per annum, as against £480 per annum in the good halls of residence at Loughborough. Even with the £90 return air fare which the Uganda Government obtains for students, it is cheaper to send them to England! In fact, the Loughborough figure no doubt reflects a large grant from the British taxpayer. Second, the existing staff salaries, at around £1,600 per annum, are going to look extremely odd in comparison with the £3,000/£4,000 tax free salaries of UNESCO staff. This latter difficulty has also arisen in connexion with the Kenya Poly-technic. Both those issues must be further considered in assessing policy more generally in later chapters.

(d) Industrial and Commercial Training

This heading deals with a wide variety of training, running from three-year residential courses to in-service training which may amount to little more than 'watching Joe'. Obviously, it is the larger organizations which can afford to run their own training centres, or to send trainees for experience with a parent company in the UK.

The biggest and best training centre is that run by East African Railways & Harbours in Nairobi for their 27,000 employees—their full training facilities in East Africa are said to have cost over £400,000 in capital and to cost upwards of £200,000 per annum to run if the wages paid to students in training are included. Other centres run by Public Utilities include those of E. A. Posts & Tele-communications (Langata), Uganda Electricity Board (Jinja), E. A. Power & Lighting (Nairobi). Among the larger firms, substantial and formalized training schemes are run by the oil companies, Gailey & Roberts, Bata Shoes, East African Tobacco, Jinja Textiles ('Nytil'), the main banks, some of the plantation companies, East African Airways and a few more companies on a smaller scale. The intake to these schemes of course varies with the job for which training is given. Operative and semi-skilled training is, of course, in-service; artisan training may be complete, but more usually is built upon a trade school qualification. Commercial and technician training will be done normally in association with the nearest technical institute, and here the intake will normally be at School Certificate level. Finally, a number of organizations seek to recruit young African graduates, either with Arts Degrees for general management or with appropriate professional qualifications, as engineers, accountants, chemists etc. There are never enough of these to go round (since so many are required for government Africanisation programmes) and most of them could have their

---

[1] Quoted by the College. The World Bank Mission quotes £385, no doubt on a different basis of calculation.

pick of half a dozen jobs for the asking. Even the boy with a good School Certificate may well be approached by the banks, railways, industrial firms and Posts & Telecommunications Department quite apart from approaches by various government departments and the East African Common Services organization.

While the larger organizations have been well aware of the need to replace at least some of their technical, executive and managerial staff by recruiting and training Africans, there are a host of smaller firms who have made little headway and sometimes little effort in this direction. They are certainly faced with great difficulties, since the larger organizations can outbid them for the small supply of candidates available and, if they are too small to run their own training, a good technical institute with appropriate courses has only recently become available in any of the three countries. On the whole, Asian staff, who frequently fill the middle technical and clerical positions, have trained themselves, and Europeans coming out to East Africa as adults are already trained. Thus to set out upon a programme of training Africans, who will be hard to find with the necessary basic qualifications, is beyond the purse and effort of many smaller firms. It is for them that the up-graded and re-organized technical institutes will be of especial value from now on.

A word should be said of the value, particularly for small employers, of the Trade Testing system and of the most useful 'Aptitude-Testing' Unit which has been established under the Ministry of Labour in Kenya, with aid and advice from the South African Institute of Personnel Administration. The Unit has done very worthwhile work in pre-selection testing for companies[1] as a guide to admission into their training schemes. It has acquired experience of applying tests in local conditions which are far more reliable than the application of tests elaborated for a UK or similar environment.

3. GOVERNMENT VOCATIONAL TRAINING

Chapter I has already emphasized how important in East Africa is the provision of training by government departments in their own training centres. The biggest of these schemes are teacher training, agricultural and veterinary, medical, Public Works Department and Police; next in size and importance would come training in Co-operation, Community Development, local government; third, there are quite a number of more specialized training schemes—forest rangers, game scouts, junior staff in the Water Department, Survey, Lands, Legal Department, Immigration, Customs & Excise, and various small miscellaneous schemes. Finally, there is a new and

---

[1] Selection testing is also done for admission of entrants to the Kenya trade schools.

important development in the shape of training for general administration, at clerical, executive and administrative levels, mainly as part of the Africanisation programmes.

In broad outline, there are four points of intake for the main schemes, now being reduced to three. First, for the junior levels, there is an intake at Standard VIII, the end of primary education. At this level a two-year training course is provided, in all three territories, for primary school teachers, the junior ranks of agricultural, veterinary and medical staff (under such names as Agricultural Assistant, Field Assistant, Veterinary Assistant, Graded Dresser, Assistant Nurse), for Police Constables (six months only), and a host of other junior staff. It is safe to say that there is already a surplus, which will soon be a massive surplus, of boys and girls with this qualification for every possible form of training. If anything, intake is likely to fall. For example, the Agricultural Departments are inclined to reduce the numbers of this third level field staff, and to improve their qualification by demanding Form 2 or even Form 4 entry.

The second level of entry was at Form 2 (Standard X). This was used by many Departments at a time when School Certificates were very rare and when there was an examination at this level before entry into Form 3. Many schools in Tanganyika terminated at Standard X. The examination has now been abolished, so that there will be few school leavers at this level, and more boys with School Certificate are becoming available.

The next level of entry is at Form 4 or School Certificate. There is some confusion of policy in East Africa about the types of training and career open to the School Certificate boy. In education, the position is fairly clearcut; two years of training post-School Certificate produces a teacher qualified to teach in the upper four Standards of the primary system and in Forms 1 and 2 of the secondary system. But in the agricultural and medical services there is, in effect, a tendency to divide the Form 4 entry into two groups. The first consists of boys or girls who either failed, achieved GCE only or got a Division III pass. These are being used in two-year training schemes to provide a better quality of third level field assistants; the recruitment of Standard VIII and X entrants is reduced accordingly.

The second group includes entrants with good Certificates, and these are being used to provide the second level of extension staff, with a training which may be from $2\frac{1}{2}$ to 4 years. This level is one of increasing importance. It includes the Assistant Agricultural Officer, Livestock Officer, Medical Assistant, and officers in the Co-operative and Community Development services who may go eventually to the top of the tree. It includes also technicians, technical assistants and most of the executive grades in the Civil Service. In agriculture it is now often referred to as the 'diploma level' and courses leading to Assistant Agricultural Officer are described as diploma courses.

Training takes place in the teacher training, agricultural, veterinary or medical training centres; in the centres specially established for local government, Community Development or Co-operative training (mainly the Jeanes Schools in Kenya, Nsamizi in Uganda, Tengeru in Tanganyika); or in the new centres for training for public administration—the Kenya Institute of Administration, Mzumbe in Tanganyika (and a government training centre opening in Dar-es-Salaam), Nsamizi in Uganda.

The third main point of intake is at university graduate level, mainly for the fully professional posts; and this normally takes the form of some kind of in-service internship or other learning period, or possibly the acquisition of a post-graduate qualification overseas. In the case of teachers, Makerere College has just discontinued a diploma course with entry at Higher School Certificate level (a three-year BEd. Degree is starting in its place) and there are proposals to start territorial courses at this level of entry in all three countries. Whether any candidates for such courses will appear was doubtful in 1962—the possession of Higher School Certificate is a good passport to an overseas Degree course if no place is offered in the three East African university colleges.

While these levels cover the main points of initial entry into government training from the public education system, it is important to emphasize that up-grading courses are at present of particular importance, and may continue to be for some time ahead. Faced by the necessity for rapid Africanisation, and by the need to improve the quality of staff, all the major departments have started up-grading schemes, or increased existing efforts. The point where these take effect is almost entirely a movement from the third to the second level of staff. Thus teachers originally recruited at Standard VIII may be up-graded to the next level, with an opportunity to complete School Certificate in the course of up-grading. Experienced third level agricultural, veterinary and medical staff may be called in for a mixture of refresher and up-grading course, and the best of them will complete the 'diploma' course and go up to the second level. In all these cases some years of experience in the field is taken as a substitute for a higher original educational qualification.

It will be clear that up-grading from the second level to the top level of fully professional posts presents extreme difficulties. The sheer requirements of scientific knowledge for the work of a qualified

doctor or veterinary surgeon or engineer makes it exceedingly hard
to re-train a man who left school at Form 4, however much practical
experience he has gained; and in most cases the profession itself is
jealous of its standards and unwilling to remit any of its formal
qualifications. The situation in *general* administration and in industry
and commerce is, of course, different and no doubt in a few years'
time men with only a secondary school background will be occupying
a good number of the most senior administrative posts in the Civil
Service, the Public Utilities and private industry.

Perhaps unfortunately, it goes without saying that most of the
government training is for Africans: Asians have little opportunity
to take part in it, save in some special spheres. Asian teachers have
their own teacher training colleges; a fair number of Asian girls
enter nursing as a career, and some Asian men enter training as
dispensers and other medical auxiliaries; the Public Works Departments also include some Asians in their training. But in agriculture
the Asians have never been admitted to play an effective part; and
since 1960 government departments have been so heavily bent on
Africanisation policies that Asians have been virtually excluded
from training for the public service (or indeed for many of the
Public Utilities) and also from promotion within it, save where no
African can possibly be found. Thus the main outlet for young
Asians is in training for the industrial and commercial economy,
through the technical institutes, where large numbers are to be
found; and in obtaining a Degree, often at private expense and often
overseas, most frequently in three professions—law, medicine and
engineering. With a Degree the Asian may be able to secure a
professional post in East Africa, or to work as a private professional
man, particularly in the next few years while Africans with full
qualifications are still scarce; and particularly outside the public
service. Moreover—and this is of high importance—he may well be
able to practise in Britain or America, at least for a few years until
the shape of things in East Africa can be more clearly seen.

4. UNIVERSITY OPPORTUNITY

Three university colleges—Makerere, the Royal College and the
University College of Dar-es-Salaam—together make up the
University of East Africa, which formally came into being in 1963.
Entry into the University is, with small exceptions, at the level of
Higher School Certificate, which is taken in the Sixth Forms of
secondary schools. There are some exceptional courses for which an
entry at Form 4 (School Certificate) will be accepted.

The courses available at the three colleges in 1962 were as follows:

(1) *Makerere*

Faculty of Arts

Departments:		Awards:	
	English		BA(General)
	Geography		London
	History		BA(Honours)
	Mathematics		London
	Economics		(English, Geography,
	Political Science		History or
	Sociology		Mathematics)
			BSc.(Economics)
			London

Faculty of Science

Departments:		Awards:	
	Botany		BSc.(General)
	Chemistry		London
	Geography		BSc.(Special)
	Mathematics		London
	Physics		(Geography or
	Zoology		Mathematics)

Faculty of Medicine

Departments:		Awards:	
	Anatomy		Licentiateship in
	Medicine		Medicine and
	Obstetrics &		Surgery (EA)
	Gynaecology		
	Paediatrics		
	Pathology		
	Medical Microbiology		
	Physiology		
	Preventive Medicine		
	Surgery		

Faculty of Agriculture

Departments:		Awards:	
	Agriculture		Diploma in
	Agricultural		Agriculture
	Biology		(EA)—to
	Agricultural		become a Degree,
	Chemistry		BSc.(Ag.)

Faculty of Veterinary Science
(to be transferred to the Royal College)

Departments:		Awards:	
	Veterinary		Diploma in
	Anatomy		Veterinary Science
	Physiology		(EA)—to become
	Pathology		a Degree)
	Animal		
	Husbandry		
	Vet. Surgery		
	& Medicine		

Faculty of Education

Departments:		Awards:	
	Education		Diploma in
	Language		Education (EA)
	Method		(A BEd. Degree
	Educational		is to start)
	Psychology		

Margaret Trowell
School of Art   Awards: Diploma in Fine Art

Department of Extra Mural Studies

(2) *The Royal College, Nairobi*

Faculty of Arts

Departments:	English	Awards: BA(General)
	Geography	London
	History	
	Economics	
	Mathematics	

Faculty of Science

Departments:	Botany	Award: BSc.(General)
	Geography	London
	Geology	
	Mathematics	
	Physics	
	Zoology	

Faculty of Engineering

Departments:	Civil	Awards: BSc.(Eng.)
	Engineering	
	Mechanical Engineering	
	Electrical Engineering	
	Land Surveying	Final Exam. RICS

Faculty of Art & Architecture

Departments:	Art	Awards: Dip. Fine Art (EA)
	Architecture	Final Exam. ARIBA
	Quantity	(Final Exam. RCS)
	Surveying	

Faculty of Special Professional Studies

Departments:	Business	Awards: Probably a BCom.
	Administration	degree
	Public Administration	(Post Graduate)
	Accountancy	(Final Exam. CIS)
	Domestic Science	(Manchester
		University Cert.)

Faculty of Veterinary Science
(to be transferred from Makerere, *q.v.*)

(3) *University College, Dar-es-Salaam*

Faculty of Law, 1962.
(*Note:* A Faculty of Arts and a Faculty of Science are planned for 1964).

ENROLMENTS, *1961–2*

	Kenya	*Uganda*	*Tanganyika*	*Zanzibar*	*Total*
Makerere	319	278	156	17	770[1]
Royal College	241	131	82	—	{ 454[2] { 415

[1] Excludes the one-year course for British and American teachers, numbering 162; 11 students from Central Africa, 1 from West Indies and 7 'Others'. Source—Annual Report.
[2] Estimated in 1961. The actual 1962 total is 415.

DIVISION BY FACULTY, 1961-2

Makerere—Arts	269	Royal College—Arts	57
Science	202	Science	59
Medicine	148	Engineering	136
Agriculture	44	Art	24
Veterinary	19	Architecture	30
Education	78	Quantity	
Fine Art	28	Surveying	8
		Land Surveying	19
	788[1] (770)	Dom. Science	34
		CIS	36
		Public	
Dar-es-Salaam		Administn.	12
(1962)—Law	20		
			415

ESTIMATED OUTPUT, 1961-5[2]

	Makerere	Royal College	Dar-es-Salaam	Total
Kenya	430	274	(5)	709
Uganda	326	120	(5)	455
Tanganyika	299	134	(10)	443[3]

STUDENTS ABROAD, 1961-2 (RETURNING BY 1966)

		Africans	Asians	Europeans
Kenya	1,368, of whom	399	664	305
Uganda	(?1,000) of whom	523	(?500)	—
Tanganyika	1,167 of whom	655	512	
			(almost wholly Asian)	

Note: The figures for 'students abroad' are extremely unreliable. They no doubt cover accurately students known to be on official scholarships and students directly sponsored by Departments, the British Council and some other foreign government programmes. But they omit a great number of private students, not only in the UK, India and the USA, where most of them are, but also in Russia and other Iron Curtain countries, to which there are various smuggling routes, notably through Ethiopia and Egypt, as well as official programmes.

The range of university opportunity looks, and is, reasonably wide. It is important to remember how recently it has come into being. Makerere opened its first General Degree courses in Arts and Science in 1950, with the first graduations in 1953. The Royal College is the transformation of the Royal Technical College, which was founded in 1954 and gained university college status only in January 1961; many of its students were originally enrolled for technical studies. The university college in Dar-es-Salaam opened its first course in borrowed buildings in 1962 and will not be a major contributor to university education until 1964, when its first main buildings are available. The large number of students overseas, both at university and diploma level, indicate the need which was felt during the 1950s for wider opportunity. To give one example, the Tanganyika Government lists 1,461 'Degrees, Diplomas and Certificates to be granted to Tanganyika students (all races), 1962-66; of these 236 will be granted in East Africa and 1,225

---

[1] *Less* Central Africa—11; 'Others'—7, i.e. 18 equals 770.

[2] Source (for Makerere and Royal College estimates) Oxford Conference on Tensions in Development. Background Paper from Uganda.

[3] This figure is about 100 higher than that estimated by the Tanganyika Manpower Survey.

Note: Figures in brackets denote approximations.

abroad'.[1] Among the subjects taken, still not offered in East Africa, are dentistry, mining, pharmacy and a large number of short, specialized courses. But the overseas list includes every subject which *is* now on offer in East Africa, and this is important. At the present time there is surplus classroom space at the Royal College and considerable surplus hostel accommodation at Makerere, mainly because *the output of students at Higher School Certificate level is insufficient to take up the places available*. On present estimates, this situation will continue until 1964, and some temporary type of course with a lower entry point may be started to use surplus space.

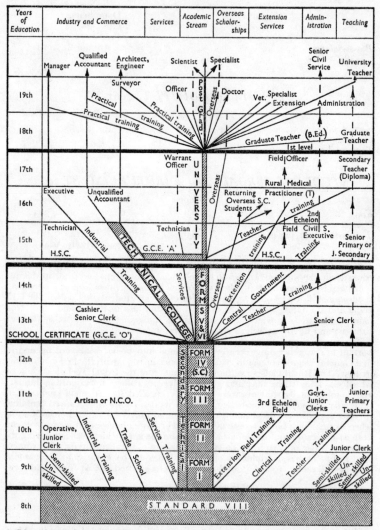

[1] 'List of Post-Secondary Students.' Prime Minister's Office, 1962. The estimate for provision in East Africa is probably too low. Some may enter in 1963 and graduate in 1966.

5. SUMMARY OF TRAINING OPPORTUNITIES

A narrative account of such varied and detailed subject matter is inevitably hard to hold in mind. The chart on the opposite page therefore attempts, though roughly, to indicate the main avenues of opportunity, showing starting points from the central school and university stream at Standard VIII, Form 4, Form 6 and at graduation. The vertical dotted lines show the possibility of up-grading, invariably implying a period of working experience in the lower grade before the up-grading course. The size of the columns is not to scale—in particular Form 1 is in reality a smaller proportion of Standard VIII and secondary technical schools are a tiny propor-tion to secondary grammar. Perhaps the two most important points to notice are that the up-grading which may take place for those who left school at Standard VIII brings them to the level of those who had an additional four years of education in a secondary school; and the vital role of the technical college in providing alternative routes both into the university and into higher technical and pro-fessional careers for boys who left school at Form 4. A considerably more detailed account of these training schemes, arranged by *subject or type of training*, as well as by entry level, is given in the following Appendix.

APPENDIX I

The following sections, set out in summary form, can be read in conjunction with the chart on p. 42 above, and give a certain incidental information about institutions and plans current in 1962. Since the chart is mainly arranged by levels, this section follows the alternative method of arrangement by subject and type of training.

A. GOVERNMENT—ADMINISTRATION, PROFESSIONAL AND EXTENSION SERVICES

(1) *Agricultural and Veterinary Services*

(a) *Post-Standard VIII or X.* It is at this level that all three Governments have in the past trained the junior ranks of the extension services, normally in a two-year course. The courses have been held at Arapai and Bukalasa in Uganda, at Embu and Siriba in Kenya and at Tengeru and Ukuriguru in Tanganyika. The numbers at this level in all three countries have been large.

Tanganyika had four levels of training. The lowest was at or below Standard VIII, and some 1,200 of these are in the field. It is proposed to allow this category to die out by natural wastage. The second category, now to be called Field Assistants, is at Standard X entry and will be raised if possible to Standard XII (School Certificate). The number now is about 1,200 and the target is about 2,000 by 1970. The training is one year on the farm followed by a two-year course. Tengeru will have an annual intake of 120 and Ukuriguru 130—total entry 250 per annum, with a minimum entry at Standard X, if possible Standard XII.

Kenya also had four levels, of which the lowest consisted in 1962 of nearly 3,000 Assistant Agricultural Instructors. The next level, usually called Agricultural or Field Assistants, number approximately 1,500, most of whom were recruited at Standard VIII, some at Form 2. These are now mainly trained in a two-year course at Embu, with a present output of 50 rising to 75 per annum.

Uganda has a smaller number, approximately 800, at the lowest level of a three-tier service. This number will probably be increased to 900 or 1,000, with the training mainly concentrated at Arapai.

All three countries have a cadre of Veterinary Assistants at a comparable level, but in smaller numbers (around 200 in Uganda, 500 in Kenya, 300 in Tanganyika). Proposals to expand the Tanganyika numbers to about 1,400 are faced by an inadequate training output of about 25 per annum.

(b) *School Certificate Entry.* All three countries are endeavouring to raise entry for the third level (described above) to School Certificate level. But simultaneously the entry to the second level course, leading to a *diploma grade* (Assistant Agricultural Officer in Kenya and Uganda, Field Officer in Tanganyika) is at a (good) School Certificate level, with a training of either $2\frac{1}{2}$ or $3\frac{1}{2}$ years.

Kenya has developed the Agricultural Diploma course both at Egerton College and at Siriba (Nyanza). It is at present a two-year course, preceded by 7 to 9 months' practical work. Siriba can turn out 25 per annum and Egerton more than double, if the veterinary course is included. The present establishment is only around 300 in Kenya, so that this rate will be excessive when Africanisation is completed by 1964/5 at this level. There is a proposal for Egerton to keep the best students on a $3\frac{1}{2}$-year course, to make them Senior AAOs, with the hope of eventually becoming AOs. On the veterinary side, the grade concerned is that of 'Livestock Officer', establishment about 120. Egerton can train students on a $2\frac{1}{2}$-year course with an output rising to 25 per annum, which would allow a considerable expansion when Africanisation is complete. About ten of the lower grade Veterinary Assistants will be sent to Kansas, USA, for a practical course, and will be up-graded to 'Assistant Livestock Officer'.

Uganda: The agricultural diploma course is at Bukulasa, with a potential output of 20 per annum, against an establishment planned to rise to just over 200. The veterinary course for the grade Assistant Veterinary Officers is at the Veterinary Training Institute, Entebbe, and is a one-year up-grading course for the best of the Veterinary Assistants, with an output of 8 per annum. There is at present no direct entry at School Certificate level.

Tanganyika: At present courses for Field Officers (diploma level) do not exist in Tanganyika. The present establishment at this level is 160, with proposed expansion to 200. Senior Field Assistants have been sent to the USA, New Zealand, Israel, Denmark, Holland, Italy, India, Pakistan. The best on return become Field Officers. A new Agricultural College is being established at Morogoro. First intake (15) will spend two years at Morogoro in 1964; thereafter the intake will be 30 per annum. Some students are taking the Egerton course (5 in 1961–3; 11 in 1962–4). Diploma-level veterinary practitioners are at present being found by promotion from Veterinary Assistants or by recruitment from abroad; some of those in post are the product of the Makerere veterinary diploma course, now discontinued.

(c) *Graduate Entry*. This grade is the full professional Agricultural or Veterinary Officer, requiring a degree and usually some post-graduate work. Entry will be via the agricultural degree at Makerere or the veterinary science degree at the Royal College. A number of Africans are at present studying abroad. In all three countries there is difficulty in filling this grade; owing to the shortage of African graduates the Veterinary Officer grade is even harder to fill.

Note: In addition to the field staff in agricultural and veterinary services, there are a considerable number of jobs, mainly with School Certificate entry, as laboratory technicians and technical assistants associated with the Agriculture, Water, Land & Surveys, Geological and similar associated Departments. Training is normally within the Department, except for senior officers.

(2) *Medical Services*

(a) *Post-Standard VIII (or X)*. There is a considerable intake for junior auxiliaries at this level in all three countries. Jobs (under various titles in the different countries) include Assistant Nurse, Graded Dresser, Darkroom Assistant, Health Assistant, Assistant Health Visitor, etc. Kenya in 1962 had in training 590 'enrolled Assistant Nurses' and another 230 trainees in other sections with Standard VIII minimum entry. Courses are mainly of two or three years.

(b) *School Certificate Entry*. There are in effect two types of training here. First, there are a number of auxiliary jobs which require at least Form 4 education, mainly owing to their technical content. These include Registered Nurses, Radiography Assistants, Physiotherapy Assistants, Laboratory Assistants, Dispensers, Health Inspectors (East Africa), and a number of other posts.

The second type concerns a grade known as Hospital Assistants (Kenya) or Medical Assistants (Tanganyika and Uganda). Originally trained from Standard X (or even VIII in earlier times) on a syllabus which concentrated mainly on *nursing* and had only a small clinical content, these men covered a wide range of duties, mainly in hospitals but also in rural centres and clinics, as assistants to a full MO. Many of the best carried out very responsible work, particularly in rural areas where the MO could only visit occasionally. As the supply of nurses has increased, and the supply of MOs has become extremely difficult, especially if the service is to be Africanised, all three countries have—(a) adopted up-grading courses for the best of the MAs, with more clinical content to the course; (b) considered (Kenya) or adopted (Uganda and Tanganyika) a course with a good School Certificate entry and much more clinical training, with the aim of producing a man capable of doing much of the simple work of a Medical Officer. Tanganyika has committed itself further: with the aid of a Rockefeller grant, the Dar-es-Salaam training centre is to produce, with SC entry and a four-year training, a cadre of 'Rural Medical Practitioners', who will in fact be rural 'GPs', with reference to full MOs for serious surgery and medical diagnosis. Some of the best Medical Assistants will be up-graded to this level. Uganda has started a three-year course at Mbale, which has something of this purpose—but the name and status of 'Assistant Medical Officer' or 'Practitioner' is being avoided. Again, Medical Assistants are being up-graded. Kenya policy was uncertain in 1962, though inclined in the same direction.

(c) *Graduate Entry*. The Makerere Degree course, associated with Mulago Hospital, has an output of about 40 per annum for East Africa, which will rise to over 60 in the next few years. This is an internationally recognized medical qualification. Until recently, Tanganyika has not been able to find enough HSC candidates to take up their quota of places on this course.

There are no training facilities in East Africa for full qualification in dentistry, pharmacy, physiotherapy, radiography, dietetics and a number of other specialisms, which must be obtained abroad. As an indication of size, the Uganda Medical Department expected, at technician level, 18 Laboratory Technicians, 4 Radiographers, 3 Physiotherapists, 10 Pharmacists, and 4 Dental Technicians to become available from training overseas in 1962-5.

(3) *Administration*

The 'Africanisation' programmes have forced all three countries to adopt a number of intensive courses for training Africans in administrative work at clerical, executive and administrative levels, and for central government, the provincial administration and local government. The main institutions are the Kenya Institute of Administration: in Tanganyika a Civil Service Training Centre (at present the Technical Institute is being used for a large number of in-service and pre-service clerical/executive courses), possibly an Institute of Public Administration, and a training centre at Mzumbe for District Officers and Assistants; in Uganda, Nsamizi College and a course in public administration run by the Department of Politics at Makerere. A good deal of this work consists of up-grading, or specially training, men with some experience whose original school qualification would be below that now required for direct entry.

Clerical Level: Entry in general is Form 4, but 'failed School Certificate' is often acceptable; many up-gradings of existing clerks, whether inside or outside government service originally.

Executive Level: Entry, School Certificate. As an example, there are about 1,050 posts (C.6-4 and C.5-2) in Kenya in the executive grade. Eleven courses of three months had been run at the KIA by the end of 1962, and from January 1963 courses of 48 School Certificate direct entrants will be run for middle grade executives.

District Assistants: This is the junior administrative grade in the provincial administration. School Certificate entry. Local government training is similar.

District Officers: Where possible, these will be graduates in future; but some have been up-graded from District Assistant level.

Senior Administrators: Graduates and in-service training, appropriate to Institutes of Public Administration.

Note: Administrative training is now at a maximum (the Kenya Institute has nearly 400 resident students and will rise to 450). It may be presumed that once Africanisation is largely completed, the system will move more towards a mixture of in-service training supplemented by up-grading and refresher courses. Courses for local government staff (and possibly for civil servants in provincial government in Kenya and elsewhere) are likely to continue for long enough.

'Senior' posts in the present administrations (i.e. down to C Scale) number 3,000–4,000 in each territory, and all these require at least School Certificate or higher educational background.

(4) *Other Departmental Training*

The next largest training Departments for government service would be the Ministry of Works, Departments of Co-operation and Community Development. On a smaller scale, training exists for a considerable number of special and mainly junior jobs—game rangers, forest rangers, water-bailiffs, etc.

Standard VIII Entry—Artisans, lowest level of field services, clerks.

School Certificate Entry—Technical and Laboratory Assistants, junior officers in Co-operatives, Community Development, etc. Senior clerks, storekeepers, Ministry of Works trainees for the Inspectorate, Assistant Quantity Surveyors and Assistant (sub-professional) grades throughout the Departments.

Graduate Entry—Engineers, Quantity Surveyors, Surveyors, professional Accountants, etc. These will be eventually drawn from the professional courses which are being developed at the Royal College.

B. TEACHER TRAINING

This has been the largest single opening for Africans with appropriate school qualifications. The nomenclature used in the territories unfortunately differs, and it may be useful to set it out here.

	Kenya	Uganda	Tanganyika
(1) *Post-Standard VIII plus 2 years training*	T4[1] or 3	Grade I[2] or II	Grade C (Post-Standard X= Grade B)
(2) *Post-School Certificate plus 2 years training*	KTI	Grade III	Grade A
(3) *Post-HSC plus 2 years at Makerere plus 2 years*	TI (Diploma)	Grade V[3] (Diploma)	Grade TI (Diploma)
(4) *Post-Graduation plus 1 year training. Post BEd. at Makerere*[4]	Graduate	Graduate	Graduate

Each country, with 10,000-plus *primary teachers* needs an intake from Standard VIII of about 750-1,000 for the two-year post-Standard VIII teacher training course to allow for something approaching 10 per cent per annum wastage and for replacing untrained teachers.

At the *post-School Certificate* level (KTI (Kenya), Grade III (Uganda) Grade A (Tanganyika)), the necessary intake is between 180 and 220 per annum. Great difficulty is now being experienced in obtaining enough candidates, and some courses are being run in which the trainee has an opportunity to take School Certificate during his teacher training course. This grade of teacher should teach in Standard V to VIII. Many are having to be used in secondary schools, Form 1 and 2, and some training colleges are considering running a special 'secondary' course for the best SC entrants.

The *TI type of teacher (Makerere Diploma)* is becoming even more difficult to find. Makerere has now ceased this course. Proposals in all three countries to run a post-HSC course for this grade (in Tanganyika at a new College at Morogoro; in Kenya probably in Nairobi; in Uganda at Kyambogo) are in danger of getting no recruits. Consideration may be given to a special three-year post-School Certificate course, to produce a new grade, and to up-grading the best of the KTI (Grade III, Grade A) teachers by an additional course, either in East Africa or in an Institute of Education in the UK.

Graduate Teachers. Asian and European schools are adequately supplied, though there is danger of a shortage in European schools owing to uncertainty of the future. African graduate teachers are desperately short. This situation is described more fully in chapter V; in brief, the number of graduates now teaching in African (or fully

---

[1] T4 were teachers who did not pass the Standard VIII examination, or a temporary grade for improved untrained teachers. Virtually in abeyance. T2 teachers are either up-graded T3 or teachers *without* School Certificate who took KTI courses from Form 4.

[2] Grade I=vernacular teachers.

[3] Starting in 1963.

[4] Grade VI=up-graded Grade III (College of Preceptors).

integrated) secondary schools is: Kenya, 440; Uganda, 240; Tanganyika, 190. The *increases* needed by 1964 are estimated at: Kenya, 230; Uganda, 210; and Tanganyika, 210. African graduates teaching in 1961–2 numbered: Kenya, 39; Uganda, 23: Tanganyika, 15. Thus for both Africanisation *and* expansion, something like 600 African graduates would be needed for Kenya, 450 for Uganda, 400 for Tanganyika, between now and 1964. There is no hope of achieving this target.

C. TECHNICAL AND COMMERCIAL—PUBLIC INSTITUTIONS

(a) *Post-Standard VIII*

Handyman or artisan training is either, at the simple level, in rural clubs and artisan centres, or at a more formal level in trade schools (6 in Kenya, 2 in Tanganyika, probably 2 in Uganda). Applications vastly exceed vacancies. Two thousand pupils completed Standard VIII in 1961 in N. Nyanza District, Kenya, for whom the trade school at Sigalagala could offer fifty places.

Secondary technical courses going to GCE are extremely few (2 in Kenya at present, 1 in Dar-es-Salaam, possibly 10 in Uganda in future).

(b) *School Certificate*

Courses to GCE(A) level are virtually confined to a single technical institute in Kampala, Nairobi and Dar-es-Salaam. A very few courses at the Royal College, Nairobi, may accept School Certificate entry. In consequence of this shortage there is bound to be a considerable volume of application for GCE(A) courses overseas, in technical colleges, as the volume of School Certificate leavers is bound to increase faster than any foreseeable expansion of the technical institutes in East Africa.

(c) *HSC Entry*

The Royal College, Nairobi, is the main point of entry at HSC level for semi-professional or fully professional technical and commercial education in such subjects as accountancy, surveying, quantity surveying, company secretaries, engineering, architecture. Here again, there is bound to be a considerable demand for overseas places in a considerable range of higher and more specialized technical training, quite apart from degree courses.

D. PROFESSIONAL

It is in the professional field that opportunities for training have been until recently most limited, especially up to the opening of full professional courses in the Royal College, Nairobi. But at the present time it is possible for an East African to attain professional status within East Africa as follows:

Doctor
Lawyer
Architect
Accountant
Company Secretary
Agricultural Officer
Veterinary Officer
Quantity Surveyor
Land Surveyor
Engineer (Electrical,
   Mechanical, Civil)

Minister of the Church
Graduate Teacher
A BCom. Degree may be started
A Diploma in Public Administration
   will soon be started
Professions requiring General or
   Honours degree in Arts or Science
   subjects taught at Makerere or
   Royal College (see syllabus)

Some estimates of *requirements* at professional level are given in chapter V. The gaps are easy to see. For example:

Pharmacy
Dental Surgery
Physiotherapy
Radiography
Dietetics
Psychology

Mining Engineering
Telecommunications
Hydraulics
Metallurgy
Journalism

and a large number of specialisms from the basic professional training, most of which are obtainable either by post-graduate work or by obtaining a higher technical qualification overseas.

E. TECHICAL AND COMMERCIAL—PRIVATE INSTITUTIONS AND PUBLIC UTILITIES

The comparatively small numbers who receive formal training within private (or Public Utility) industrial and commercial institutions, to clearly defined levels, reflects the small degree of industrialization in East Africa and the small size of most of its commercial system, largely operated by family firms within the Asian communities. There is, however, a range of training available in the larger units which includes—

(a) in-service training for semi-skilled operatives;
(b) foreman training;
(c) artisan apprenticeship;
(d) clerical training;
(e) technician training—in association with a technical institute;
(f) commercial training, accountancy, etc. also aided by a technical institute;

(g) professional training associated with the universities in East Africa and overseas;

(h) management training, mainly in-service.

The distribution of skills and types of training naturally depend upon the type of undertaking. The following list is only to be regarded as a *sample*—not all training schemes are included (though the biggest are) and not all elements in individual schemes are mentioned.

East African Railways & Harbours (major residential centre, Nairobi, Locomotive Training Centre, Railway Workshops, Dar-es-Salaam).

Training is given for artisans, technicians, clerical grades, inspectors, station staff, catering staff, engineering students; in fact, to all functions on the system.

East African Posts & Telecommunications (major training centre, Langata, Nr. Nairobi).

East African Power & Lighting & TANESCO (major centre, Nairobi; minor centre, Dar-es-Salaam).

Uganda Electricity Board[1] (residential centre, all main grades, Jinja).

East African Tobacco Company[2] (residential centre, Nairobi). In-service training at Dar-es-Salaam and Jinja factories.

Gailey & Roberts[3] (artisan training centre, Nairobi). A variety of in-service training schemes for supervision and junior management.

Other commercial companies (e.g. Smith McKenzie, Twentsche, Old East Africa Trading Company, Wigglesworth, etc.) have, in varying degrees, in-service training for their secretarial and commercial staff.

Bata Shoe Company. Considerable in-service and technical training at Limuru, Kenya.

Shell Company[4] (small residential management training centre, Nairobi). Technical training for Mombasa Refinery. Artisan training in Dar-es-Salaam.

Caltex. Operative and artisan training, and some management trainees.

Banks. All the major banks (mainly Barclays DCO, Standard Bank, National & Grindlays Bank, Ottoman Bank) have training schemes both at clerical level and at School Certificate

---

[1] Higher training may be supplemented by UK training centres and attachments.
[2] *Ibid.*
[3] *Ibid.*
[4] *Ibid.*

entry, associated with professional examinations and often with temporary attachments to UK branches or training centres.

Nyanza Textiles. Intensive operative, supervisory and technical training associated with the main factory.

Kilembe Copper Mine, Uganda. In-service training at Kilembe.

Uganda Company. In-service training for estate managers, technical and commercial staff.

Uganda Development Corporation. Some sub-sections, e.g. Uganda Hotels, have small specialized training schemes for particular grades.

Brooke Bond and other Tea Plantations
Uganda Sugar Plantations (Mehta, Madhvani and others)
Sisal Plantation Companies
Coffee Plantation Companies
Kilimanjaro Native Co-operative Union
Victoria League (Cotton Co-operative) & other large Co-operatives
Kenya Farmers' Union
Unga (Flour Milling). *Chande Industries* (Milling)
Other plantation, agricultural and processing enterprises.

In all cases the larger undertakings have some form of local or in-service training, mainly for field supervisors and for assistant Estate Managers, in some cases (particularly the Co-operatives) for secretarial, clerical and accounting work. The mills have in-service, artisan and technical training according to their needs.

In general, it would be fair to say that all the large undertakings can easily recruit boys or girls of Standard VIII level; and that, equally, all of them find it extremely difficult to recruit at School Certificate level; the competition at higher levels, for boys with Higher Certificate or with Degrees, is intense, and largely frustrated by the acute shortage of supply. The quality of training at all levels will be improved greatly as the three technical institutes expand in size and in the range of courses offered. At the management level, the Royal College, Nairobi, is anxious to develop courses and some useful work has been done by the staff over the last few years. But any larger expansion must await the time when more Africans have accumulated longer experience in the middle ranges of industry and commerce and are ready for more advanced training.

PART II

POLICY ISSUES

CHAPTER IV

THE PUBLIC NEED—MANPOWER
REQUIREMENTS

In approaching problems of policy, it is necessary to define what interests are assumed to be decisive. For there are at least three contenders—the State, with its political aims; the individual, with his private desires and ambitions; and some belief or theory as to the proper role of education, which may conflict with both. This chapter is essentially concerned with the situation as seen by African Governments. In chapters VIII and IX individual motives and educational values will be brought into the picture.

It may well be true that the most vital task facing African governments is to make some new and large provision for the great numbers of young people, who, in the next few years, will complete primary education by about the age of fourteen and will find no place in the existing secondary school programme. They are potentially the biggest source of social and, indeed, political unrest. But not only is this problem largely outside the scope of this study; it is not in itself the issue to which African governments are likely as yet to give highest priority. For their main preoccupation is to find and train enough Africans to replace expatriates in the public service, at least to take a hand in the private sector, and to direct and administer their programmes of economic development. Above all, therefore, it is the output from secondary schools which matters; for it is those with secondary education who can go on to become university graduates or receive technical or sub-professional training in a wide range of public and economic services.

How much trained manpower, at what levels and for what functions, do these three East African countries need? By courtesy of the Provisional Council of the University of East Africa, the estimates of a manpower assessment made for the Council in the summer of 1962[1] are here used to give at least a rough indication of the answer.

The first stage in a manpower assessment is to reach some estimate of the existing stock, at defined levels of responsibility and skill. The estimates for East Africa were divided into two categories.

---

[1] G. Hunter and F. H. Harbison, *High-Level Manpower in East Africa: A Preliminary Assessment*, 1962.

Category I includes the highest level—professional men of graduate or equivalent level, senior administrators, senior managers in industry and commerce. Category II includes the next layer—technicians and sub-professional grades (for example, the second echelon in agricultural extension work), executive grades in the Civil Service, middle management in industry and commerce, teachers with secondary education but without a university Degree. Broad estimates of the existing stock as at mid-1961, were as follows:

		Africans	Asians	Europeans	Total
KENYA	Cat. I	533	3,519	5,361	9,413
	Cat. II	4,679	12,710	8,894	26,283
	Total	5,212	16,229	14,255	35,696
UGANDA	Cat. I	648	1,429	2,055	4,132
	Cat. II	3,346	4,975	2,270	10,591
	Total	3,994	6,404	4,325	14,723
TANGANYIKA	Cat. I	598	1,947	1,932	4,477
	Cat. II	3,870	6,418	2,377	12,665
	Total	4,468	8,365	4,309	17,142
TOTAL, EAST AFRICA (round figures)		13,700	31,000	22,900	67,500

The heavy reliance on Europeans and Asians, and the thicker layer of senior men in Kenya compared to Uganda and Tanganyika, is evident from these figures. A third category, consisting of clerks, artisans, and the third echelon of extension services, might have been added: here the African proportion is far higher, and the European almost nil.

Second, to make a forward estimate of requirements, the first step is to make some assumptions about the rate of 'wastage'—i.e. the numbers now in post who will die, or retire or leave the country within the period under review. These wastages were estimated for 1961–1966 and 1966–1971. A very high figure (80 per cent in the first five years) was estimated for European wastage from government service to take account of 'Africanisation'; a much lower figure (40 per cent in the public service, 25 per cent in the private sector) was taken for Asians; and a low figure (15 per cent–20 per cent) for Africans mostly young and newly appointed.

The third step is to estimate what numbers of trained men will be needed by each economy to allow for growth. There are two elements in this estimate. First, some assumption as to over-all growth of national income; second, a translation of this growth into manpower needs at various levels. Experience indicates that, if national income is growing at, say, 4 per cent per annum, double this rate must be allowed for growth in Category I and treble in Category II—for eventually there should be about five technicians to every graduate. Unfortunately, on the other hand, 4 per cent national income growth probably does not mean more than 1 per cent–1.5 per cent growth in *total* wage employment, and possibly 4 per cent at the artisan/clerical level.

On these assumptions, the actual estimates for the first five years (1961–66) gave two alternative results—one based on a prospect of slow growth—about 2 per cent per annum—and one on a more optimistic estimate—about 3 per cent per annum. These are, indeed, modest hopes of economic growth; but they covered a period of transition to independence in which investment was hesitant and depressed.

	(1) Stock 1961	(2) Wastage 1961–66	(3) Growth (a) 2 per cent p.a.	(3) Growth (b) 3 per cent p.a.	(4) Requirement (a)	(4) Requirement (b)
KENYA						
Cat. I	9,400	3,750	1,900	2,800	5,650	6,550
Cat. II	26,300	8,900	7,900	11,800	16,800	20,700
Total					22,450	27,250
UGANDA						
Cat. I	4,150	1,600	830	1,250	2,430	2,850
Cat. II	10,600	3,000	3,180	4,800	6,180	7,800
Total					8,610	10,650
TANGANYIKA						
Cat. I	4,480	1,600	890	1,350	2,500	2,950
Cat. II	12,700	3,650	3,810	5,700	7,500	9,350
Total					10,000	12,300

Note: 'Requirement'=Wastage + Growth, at the lower (a) or higher (b) level.

It is worth noting that, on these assumptions of wastage and growth, and over five years, roughly one Category I to three Category II men are needed to come forward, which indicates that about a quarter of those who pass School Certificate should go on to university or similar training, and three quarters should enter vocational training at once.

If a further projection, on the same lines, is carried forward to 1971 (with all the reservations possible about its accuracy or usefulness) the figures for Requirements would be (assuming a 4½ per cent growth as the 'high' figure):

REQUIREMENTS 1966–1971

		(a) *2 per cent per annum growth*	(b) *4½ per cent per annum growth*
KENYA	Cat. I	4,400	7,700
	Cat. II	17,000	32,300
	Total	21,400	40,000
UGANDA	Cat. I	2,000	3,500
	Cat. II	6,900	13,100
	Total	8,900	16,600
TANGANYIKA	Cat. I	2,160	3,780
	Cat. II	8,250	15,670
	Total	10,410	19,450

Note: The proportion of Category II to Category I is growing larger—up to 4½ to 1—as the differential rate of growth takes effect.

These estimates represent orders of magnitude—no crystal ball is good enough to give accuracy. But they do represent targets for educational planning which would make sense. Some targets must be set, because the process of education is so long that a decision to establish a secondary school does not produce a university graduate until about nine years from the opening of Form 1.

While over-all figures give a target for the total size of the secondary and higher educational system, they do not, of course, indicate how many teachers or engineers or doctors are needed. To obtain these figures quite separate estimates, sector by sector, have to be made. This is in a sense far more difficult, at least for certain sectors; for it involves estimating not merely a *general* rate of growth for the economy but a particular rate for particular functions—e.g. engineering or building. The levels suggested in the assessment, for an annual output, sufficient both to maintain and substantially to improve the manning of certain professions in East Africa, were as follows:

ANNUAL OUTPUT TARGETS—GRADUATES

	1966–71	*1971 onwards*
Agriculture ⎫		
Veterinary ⎬	155	195
Supporting Scientists ⎭		
Graduate Teachers	75	100
Engineers	40–50	75–100
Doctors	40–50	60
Lawyers	30–40	40–60
Other General Science	200	300
Other Arts	200	300
	740–770	1,070–1,115

These figures do not assume that East Africa would suddenly reach the manning position of a fully developed society in less than ten years. They are based partly on what the countries may be able to produce in terms of candidates qualified for university studies and partly on what the economies are likely to be able to employ and pay on any conceivable estimate of economic growth. Thus, the present estimates of HSC passes in 1963–1967 total about 3,500 for the five years: and this would make possible a university (or equivalent) five-year output of 3,500 three years later, i.e. between 1966–1971. The estimate of 750 per annum given in the table—i.e. 3,750 in five years—is thus a little higher.

There are a number of features of these estimates which are worth a moment's consideration. Over half the requirement is put in General Science and Arts Degree. The reason for this is to maintain a vital flexibility. There are very many different professions and functions for which a first Degree in Science or Arts provides a basis —not least the central Civil Service and the higher ranges of management. It is impossible, and undesirable, to forecast how many students should take economics, or specialized branches of science. There are many particular directions in which the economy may develop, and nothing is more dangerous than to provide for *specialized* training far ahead—the industry which would use metallurgists or ciné-technicians may not be founded or fail to expand. Higher education provides a platform from which many specialisms can be developed, often with only a year or two of post-graduate work.

Second, the provision for doctors is small, and for lawyers even smaller. There are two reasons for this. First, if a country is determined upon maximum growth in minimum time, there are some sacrifices to be made. A full Welfare State cannot be built without *first* developing a high national income. While a considerable improvement in medical services is certainly a condition for higher productivity, medical needs could easily swallow up all the high-level manpower needed for the agriculture and industry which earn the national income; and there is plenty of precedent for a surplus of lawyers, with a dearth of scientists, in other growing countries. Their law and medicine are perhaps the most popular choices for the 'unplanned' student, who goes abroad at his family's expense to become qualified. East Africa certainly need never lack Asian lawyers and Asian doctors, trained largely at private expense, and willing to enter private practice if opportunity offers. The provision made in these tables is simply to man the *public* medical and legal services. It is necessary to add that, in the past, there has been some difficulty in keeping trained doctors and lawyers in the public service, owing to the monetary attractions of private practice.

Finally, relatively high figures are given for agriculture and teaching. The reason is clear. Agriculture (all forms of husbandry) is the foundation of these economies, and the area in which by far the greatest increases of productivity could be achieved. Those increases depend partly upon science, but much more upon education of the peasant population. It is the secondary schools which will produce the teachers and the agricultural extension staff, and it is on these two groups that economic growth in East Africa must depend.

CHAPTER V

THE PUBLIC NEED—SUPPLY FROM
EDUCATION AND TRAINING

The sources of supply to meet the requirements roughly assessed
in chapter IV are the new output from secondary schools in East
Africa, and of universities, technical colleges and other post-
secondary training institutions either in East Africa or overseas.
The second main source lies in men and women already employed
in East Africa in positions below Category II who can be up-graded,
by suitable training, to take higher responsibilities. While most of
the argument in this chapter deals with the new output, this resource
of adult and experienced staff is of great importance. Many of them
might well have had the ability to profit from secondary or even
university education had it been available in their day; full use of
their potential may make a great difference to the success of African
governments in meeting the challenge which they have set themselves.

For the period 1961–1966, the output from secondary education
and university colleges in East Africa is not hard to assess, since
those taking School Certificate in 1966 must enter secondary education in 1962, and those graduating in 1966 must also already be
inside the secondary schools by 1962, if they are not already within
a university.

ESTIMATED OUTPUT, SECONDARY EDUCATION, 1961–1965

	SC Entrants	Passes Div. I & II	Passes Div. III or GCE	Fail
Kenya	19,300	8,750	5,800	4,750
Uganda	9,000	6,500[1]	1,000	1,500
Tanganyika	15,000	7,000	3,000	5,000[2]

Note: [1] 6,500 includes Div. III.
[2] The proportion of failures is higher than for Kenya and Uganda, but
lower than local estimates.

Taking the Kenya figures first, and subtracting 2,100 HSC
entrants from the Division I & II passes, there are left 6,650 Division
I & II passes and 5,800 Division III or GCE passes. This total
(12,450) contains 2,000 Europeans, of whom not more than 500
might be likely to enter the economy. The total available for on-
training at School Certificate level is therefore about 11,000, to

63

which the 4,750 failures might be added. The racial distribution of passes would be roughly African 5,850; Asian 4,600; European 550.

In Uganda, after deducting HSC entry, about 5,500 SC and GCE passes will be available, with about 1,500 failures. In Tanganyika, a similar calculation gives a figure of 8,200.

At the graduate level, a somewhat complicated estimate of students graduating both in East Africa and overseas suggests that about 2,500 may become available to Kenya in the five-year period, 700 to Uganda[1] and 1,650 to Tanganyika.

The table below compares the Requirements, estimated in chapter IV, with these anticipated sources of supply. The supply figures for the second five years—1966–1971, calculated in a similar way, have been added to the table.

HIGHER MANPOWER—REQUIREMENTS AND SUPPLY

	1961–1966 Lower R	1961–1966 Higher R	1961–1966 Supply	1966–1971 Lower R	1966–1971 Higher R	1966–1971 Supply
KENYA						
Cat. I	5,650	6,550	2,500	4,400	7,700	5,000
Cat. II	16,800	20,700	11,000	17,000	32,300	21,000
Total	22,450	27,250	13,500	21,400	40,000	26,000
UGANDA						
Cat. I	2,430	2,850	700[2]	2,000	3,500	1,500
Cat. II	6,180	7,800	5,850[3]	6,900	13,100	8,500
Total	8,610	10,650	6,550	8,900	16,600	10,000
TANGANYIKA						
Cat. I	2,500	2,950	1,650	2,160	3,780	2,000
Cat. II	7,500	9,350	8,200	8,250	15,670	12,000
Total	10,000	12,300	9,850	10,410	19,450	14,000

Once again, these figures are necessarily rough orders of magnitude. But they indicate, for each of the three countries, two or three major conclusions. First, no country in 1961–1966 can meet both wastage and even the lowest rate of growth from the output of secondary schools in East Africa, *whether or not* those who pass School Certificate go overseas for university or other courses. Even if those who fail School Certificate and do not even get a GCE pass had been included as 'Supply', only Tanganyika could reach the requirement figures. On the other hand, in 1966–1971 the

---

[1] This figure excludes Asians studying abroad, and might be increased by as much as 500.

[2] *Ibid.*

[3] 350 added to the figure of 5,500 given above, to cover students returning from overseas with diploma or other non-graduate qualifications.

output from secondary schools, greatly increased, could reach the lower requirement, though it still falls short of the higher figure. This conclusion is to be expected, for it is hardly likely that any country, in the five years 1961–1966, could both replace nearly all its Europeans and a large number of Asians from senior levels in the economy and also expand its stock. The strain is far less from 1966 onwards, because the main replacement effort is over, and the new intake can be devoted much more to expansion.

The second important conclusion is that the supply of graduates for Category I manpower (these are not synonymous: probably not more than 60 per cent of Category I need be graduates) is even harder to find than a supply for Category II. This is because the graduate takes longer to train, so that the effects of expanding secondary education are felt only after a longer delay.

Both conclusions lead to a further clear inference—that the shortfall will have to be made good in each country by some new recruitment of expatriate 'experts', on contract, to fill the gaps, and particularly those in Category I for graduate professional men.

These are conclusions which are unpalatable to African governments, and there are necessarily pressures to avoid or reverse them, which in turn may give rise to changes in education policy. Before turning to some of these pressures, it may be as well to look at the supply position, in relation to requirements, in one or two key sectors of the economy.

(a) *Medical*

In 1961–2 there were just under 300 qualified Medical Officers in the public service in the three countries put together. In addition, there were between 1,100 and 1,200 in private practice, mainly Asians. Not more than about sixty doctors in the public service were Africans, and the numbers in private practice were smaller still. In these circumstances, it is likely that a first aim of African governments would be to 'Africanise' the public service. An output of forty doctors per annum, giving 200 in five years, would go a long way to achieve this, and would ultimately sustain a cadre of nearly 800, if wastage by death and retirement is calculated at 5 per cent per annum (i.e. a 20-year life in the job). This is a level which Makerere could well sustain, and indeed could increase by 1970, if not before, to an output of 60 per annum; sustaining a cadre of 1,000–1,200. Although, therefore, in the short term there is a severe shortage of African doctors (and nothing can be done to create them, as fully qualified MOs, out of thin air), in the longer term the public service at least should be African, if that is so desired, well before 1970.

But at the lower levels, where Africanisation is still not very far advanced, a higher output is very desirable. Moreover, there are

F

many skills for which training is not available in East Africa—
pharmacy, full physiotherapy and radiography qualifications, and
several more. In these areas overseas training is clearly necessary
until the gaps are filled in East Africa.

However, even a doubling of the present strength of the public
service may well seem inadequate in countries where infant mor-
tality is high and where preventable disease and parasitic infestation
is so common. To take one example, no country in East Africa has a
school medical service (or dental or optical service) and thousands
of children struggle through school life burdened by bilharzia,
malaria, unrelieved short sightedness, and many other debilitating
handicaps.

It is in this connexion that the bold decision of Tanganyika to train
'Rural Medical Practitioners' (four years from SC entry) has so much
to commend it. These men, working in remote rural areas, can give
a degree of medical service to the huge rural population which
could not possibly be afforded if treatment were confined to fully
qualified MOs. There would not be such reason for concern at
having only 100 MOs in a country if there were 600 of these
assistants to support them. There may well be a case, in all three
countries, for increasing the numbers in training, which at present
are running only at about 30 per year in Tanganyika and 15 in
Uganda at Mbale, in addition to the stock of up-graded Standard
VIII or X Medical Assistants. The chart on p. 42 shows what a
great gap must exist between the Standard VIII entrant and the
School Certificate entrant, and the process of upgrading can only
overcome this for men of outstanding quality.

(b) Agricultural and Veterinary Services

The stock of fully qualified Agricultural Officers runs at over 100
in Kenya, 50 in Uganda, 70 in Tanganyika. All three countries
have reasonable prospects of finding Africans for these posts in
about six to eight years. But here again a strengthening of the
service can most quickly be achieved by adding to the second
echelon, the Field Officer of diploma training (School Certificate
plus three years). Numbers at present are Kenya 288; Uganda 142;
Tanganyika 162. A proportion of 75 graduates to 300 or even 400
diplomates would be feasible, because the supply at School Certificate level will be there, while the supply of graduates will not.

On the veterinary side, the position is far worse. None of the
three countries have an adequate supply of graduate African
Veterinary Officers in sight to man the top posts (Kenya 50, Uganda
33, Tanganyika 66). Moreover, the second echelon, Livestock
Officers, is still small, except in Kenya (160 at this level); proposals
in Uganda and Tanganyika are for increases from 40 to 60 and from

63 to 70 respectively. Here again, there is room for much expansion at the 'diploma' level, at present hampered by professional trade unionism among the qualified Veterinary Officers. Expansion means another call on School Certificate entrants, and better training facilities.

(c) *Engineers*

The professional Institute records about 150 civil and municipal engineers and 205 electrical engineers in East Africa. This figure does not include some Asians with qualifications obtained in India, and of course omits mechanical, mining and chemical engineers, who probably account for another 500.[1] To maintain a force of 750–1,000 engineers would need an annual output of fifty. At present, the number of qualified African engineers is well under fifty in East Africa, and the experience of training them at the Royal College has been unfortunately unsuccessful. This is neither due to an inherent incapacity of Africans—that well-worn myth—nor to failure by the teaching staff. It is fundamentally due to the weakness of science teaching in the schools, so that entrants to an engineering Degree come in ill-prepared to take it. The remedy may well be to insist, save in exceptional cases, that aspirants to Degree training should do at least two and possibly three years at the Polytechnic engineering course, from School Certificate, so that those with aptitude and ability can enter the Degree course properly prepared, while those with less theoretical aptitude can continue along a practical line to the Ordinary or Higher Certificate. This is another case where university provision has suffered because it was prematurely imposed on a system of secondary and technical education which needed more time to develop in quality, equipment and teaching staff.

(d) *Scientists*

There is always a danger that concentration on professional training (medicine, agriculture, engineering) will weaken the effort in straight scientific teaching. East Africa is extremely short of scientists, perhaps especially on the biological side, because the obvious professions attract African and Asian entrants so strongly. The future position is not unhopeful, because the tendency in African secondary schools is for more students to opt for the Science than the Arts course in the Sixth Form—this was true in almost every one of the forty secondary schools visited in 1962. The first necessity is to improve science teaching, and the small Ford Foundation team in Nairobi, which has been running courses for science

---

[1] EAR & H alone would account for over 200 mechanical and civil engineers.

teachers, has made an excellent start, especially in inventive suggestions for cheap home-made equipment of the string-and-jampot variety which can be used for effective demonstration and can save huge sums of money. The laboratories in secondary schools are not at all to be despised: teaching is the crux. Here one major problem of developing countries is contained *in parvo*: for they need above all just those skills in science and in teaching upon which the developed—but still frantically developing—countries themselves rely. It is a job to get a good biologist for British schools, let alone to spare them for Africa. The programme for recruiting teachers for the overseas countries has got to develop far more energy, and spread far more widely, if the need is to be met. For, even if it were desirable to bring boys of fourteen to Britain for a scientific secondary course, the numbers and cost involved makes it impossible; and at higher levels the lack of proper foundations shows all too clearly.

(e) *Teachers*

The programme for expansion of secondary schools in East Africa depends upon the availability of graduate teachers. The published estimates of need are:

GRADUATE TEACHERS FOR SECONDARY SCHOOLS
(African or Integrated)

	Stock 1961	Required 1964	Wastage 1961–5 (8 per cent p.a.)	Total Required
Kenya	440	670	130	360
Uganda	240	450	75	285
Tanganyika	190	400	60	270
	870	1,520	265	915

If these figures were projected on to 1966, allowing further expansion and some wastage (there is an inevitable wastage of two-year contract expatriate teachers, and of many expatriates who were on the regular staff) the requirement would certainly rise to 1,200 and probably higher still. Teachers, for better or for worse, supply many other, better paid, professions with recruits, and this has been particularly true in tropical Africa, where parliaments and the Civil Service have been so largely manned by them. Here, therefore, a high wastage rate from this sector to others must be assumed—the 8 per cent given above, implying a $12\frac{1}{2}$ year professional stint, should probably be raised to at least 10 per cent and possibly higher. To maintain a stock of even 1,500 graduate teachers would thus mean an annual output of 150 per year. To meet this, the proposed BEd. course at Makerere will produce thirty per year, and the courses designed territorially for HSC entry will be lucky if they recruit twenty students annually, at least until after 1964. Thus the output in East Africa is far below clearly anticipated demand; the shortfall can only be met by importing expatriates, partly under the Teachers for East Africa scheme (Anglo-American) which resulted from the 1960 Princeton Conference, and by any and all other methods. The basic problem is the lack of incentives comparable to those which are now available to African graduates in the Civil Service and in industry, with prospects of headlong promotion under Africanisation programmes; and this same incentive problem is shrinking the intake of teacher-trainees at the School Certificate level.

These figures have covered only the needs in secondary institutions; three university colleges, three technical institutes, and many other institutions are still reliant upon expatriate staff and anxious to find African substitutes soon.

This grave situation is not, after all, surprising. The over-all figures of manpower requirements and supply showed a large deficit, and that deficit must show up in some actual sector. It shows in the secondary teaching sector for obvious incentive reasons; and it cannot be banished by the wave of a wand or by a new party in power.

(f) *General*

These brief comments on the total supply, and the sector supply, of African manpower to staff growing and changing societies emphasize again and again the same three points. First, that the expansion of secondary schools is the key to the whole situation. Second, that for the next five years or more strategy must be to make the best use of Form 4 boys and girls to man vital services after a three-year training to diploma or equivalent level—university graduates are simply not available nor is a university Degree so widely essential as perhaps the British Administration used to insist. Third, that the key contribution from outside East Africa is in providing teaching staff, and notably scientists. It is as well to stress these three points before turning, in the next two chapters, to another form of aid—the provision of scholarships overseas.

CHAPTER VI

THE PUBLIC NEED—THE CASE FOR OVERSEAS TRAINING

There is one wide assumption which must qualify the following discussion of training Africans overseas. It is the assumption that secondary education, up to Form 4 (SC or GCE) should take place in East Africa; that it is uneconomic and impractical for the State to embark upon secondary education overseas, even if a few richer individuals are prepared to send and pay for their children in overseas schools.

We are therefore concerned with the case for overseas training at four levels:

(a) for some experienced adults, whatever their first educational level;

(b) for students leaving Form 4 (i.e. at age 18 to 20);

(c) for students leaving Form 6 (i.e. at age 20 to 22);

(d) post-graduate training (i.e. at age 23 to 27).

There appear to be five main reasons why it might be good policy to send or assist students to go abroad. They are as follows:

(a) no places available, at their level, in East Africa, irrespective of subject;

(b) places available, but at a distance, without accommodation;

(c) places available in the subject, but training unsuitable or inferior;

(d) special subject not taught in East Africa;

(e) value of overseas training regarded as paramount, outweighing cost, even if training is, or could be made, available in East Africa.

These five possible cases may be considered in turn.

(a) *No Places Available*

At the present moment, the university colleges could take more entrants than are available at the level of a Higher School Certificate pass. This argument does not, therefore, apply if the entry qualifications remain unaltered. It is probably true that the colleges could not take all those who completed the HSC course *including* those who fail the examination. But it is in any case unlikely that all would want or benefit from a Degree course, and there are more than enough opportunities for further training—particularly in industry, teaching, government service, either central, local or field extension.

The case is, however, stronger at Form 4 level. It is certainly arguable that the virtual exclusion of all but Division I plus 30 per cent of Division II passes from entry to the Sixth Forms in schools is unduly restrictive. There must be at least some boys or girls who did poorly in the examination but are well worth further academic education. Some of them may turn out better than some who got Division I passes. This argument would not be accepted at the present day by all Headmasters. Some of those interviewed felt that, under government pressure, they had accepted many more candidates into an HSC course than had any hope of completing it with credit or profit to themselves. Nevertheless, the bottleneck between Form 4 and Forms 5 and 6 is at present too narrow; it might be that a larger admission to Form 5 should take place and that the weaker candidates, as judged at the end of a year's Fifth Form work, should be transferred to other forms of training. A different suggestion is that there should be another, academic, choice at Form 4, as an alternative to entering the HSC course—a 'Junior College'. This is considered below (Section c).

(b) *Places Available; Difficulties of Distance, Eligibility, etc.*

The secondary schools and university colleges are residential (except for Asian schools), and there is therefore no great difficulty for candidates from remote areas accepting places. School fees may be a problem: but the District or Provincial Councils are at present generous in their grants to deserving candidates. If the day comes when local finances cannot meet this charge, a government decision will be needed. But at present it would rarely, if ever, be true to say that a boy or girl with School Certificate needs an overseas scholarship because of inability to pay secondary or university fees. Where such cases exist, the remedy is not, in any case, to send them abroad, but to increase grants within East Africa.

The case is stronger in relation to technical college studies. A full range of technical courses is only available in the three capital cities, and the hostel accommodation is limited in all of them. In places such as Jinja and Mbale in Uganda; Kisumu, possibly Kericho, Nyeri and Thika in Kenya: and Mwanza, Tanga and possibly Arusha in Tanganyika there would seem to be a case at least for a small, high-grade Evening Institute, with some day courses, for those students who either cannot get a place in a hostel in the central technical college or for whom prolonged absence on a full-time course is next to impossible. Naturally, this provision would have to bear a relation to the number of jobs at technician level likely to become available. Although it would be cheaper than subsidized residential hostels, it would be expensive in staff, teaching small classes in a range of subjects. However, this provision is not made at present and would take time to set up. Meanwhile, there is a case for at least some overseas places in technical education at Form 4, for boys who cannot use the central institutions.

A further case might be made for young people who refused, or could not get or take, a place in higher education at the moment when they left Form 4 but subsequently, after perhaps two years in a job, could and would accept and benefit from it. These cases are probably numerous in East Africa. They certainly cannot get re-admission to the HSC course in secondary schools, nor would this be suitable; they are not eligible for entrance to the East African university colleges, and they may not be technically inclined or able to enter a technical college. The College of Social Studies (Kikuyu, Kenya) can accept about twelve such students for a one-year further course of study, and it will be of interest to observe both the number of candidates and the results of this work. But this is a very minor provision. The main opportunity at present in East Africa would be to enter vocational training—in agriculture, medical services, central government or industry and commerce—and this is by no means an unreasonable answer. It does not, however, meet the case of a young man or girl who is determined to pursue more academic work but fell off the ladder at Form 4 for a multitude of possible reasons.

(c) *Places Available, Syllabus Unsuitable*

This case is by far the most difficult to assess clearly, and raises major policy issues. In broad outline, the case is that the present offer of a place in an HSC course in a secondary school, prepar-atory to university entrance, is not only inadequate in numbers (this was dealt with in Section (a) on p. 70) but unsuitable for at least some possible entrants *who have the capacity to benefit from higher general education*: if they have not this capacity, there is a wide range of vocational training which they can enter at Form 4, and the argu-ment collapses. The argument can be put in three main ways. First, that boys and girls of eighteen to twenty years of age are too old to stay at school: second that the school environment is too poor in physical equipment, food, etc.; third that the standard of teaching is not good enough. These are arguments against the provision of Fifth and Sixth Forms in schools, as such.

The last two arguments will not stand up to much criticism. If the standard of teaching is poor, how is some other institution to improve on it, without stealing the very teachers now in the schools or needed by them? If the alternative institution is to be on college or university lines, there is little likelihood of university lecturers, if they are obtainable, having the skill or the time to give the personal attention to these school certificate entrants which can be given by a teacher skilled in and fond of this type of work. Sixth Form teaching is a vocation as much, if not more, than university teaching, and it is entirely different in its whole style and approach. It is being justified at present by achieving a considerably higher proportion of HSC passes from the schools than was obtained from the Makerere pre-university course, although the latter drew upon the whole of East Africa for its entry.

As to the argument on environment, this goes back ultimately to the financial strength and whole standard of living of East African countries. It is certainly possible to set up a 'Sixth Form College', such as the Catholic Strathmore College in Nairobi, for a few HSC students—Strathmore has 120 places—at a high standard of buildings, equipment and food. But when the present tiny trickle of candidates becomes a full stream, many such colleges would be needed. Are they to be specially built, on new sites, with new access roads, power, drainage, common services, libraries? If so, it will be an exceedingly costly undertaking. It costs over £300 per year per boy at Strathmore. Fees are £60 per year, and every African boy is on a bursary to meet them. Would it not be better to add a building or two on the sites of the best of the existing secondary schools, where water, roads, light, chapel, hall, library, etc. already exist? If so, how will they differ from existing Sixth Forms, save in detail? In fact, experience in the existing schools seems to be that it is a mistake to separate the Sixth Form group from the main school, if it is on the site at all, and that after three to four years, if not less, the Sixth Form provides a natural climax to a secondary school career, gives leadership (and the experience of leadership) to the school, invigorates the lower school work, and attracts a better quality of teacher, whether expatriate or not. Headmasters interviewed were, without a single exception, convinced that the impact of Sixth Form work was creating a revolutionary change in the quality of secondary education. For the first time (however regrettable this may be) boys were really being taught to think, to read intelligently instead of memorizing, to select, to marshal argument, to evaluate. The importance of this change surely needs no emphasis.

The argument on age is more important. Until very recently, many boys did not reach Form 4 until the age of twenty or even higher; and it is certainly awkward to insist that a young man of twenty should continue as a 'schoolboy' for yet another two years, while his contemporaries in Britain or America would be completing their Degree course, entered at 18, at the age of 21 or 22. Particularly is this true in a newly independent country, set upon rapid advance, urgently needing able young men, offering employment to Form 4 leavers which may give them a salary of £700 per annum in two years. However, Africans have not been so self-conscious about exact years of age (not always clearly known in any case), and discontent at remaining at school has arisen mainly by *comparison*. Until 1959 the Sixth Form was, in effect, the Makerere pre-university course, with its environment of university buildings, gowns, better food, pocket money, freedom and adulthood. It was certainly a come-down to remain, instead, at school. Moreover, some overseas scholarships, and some places in the Royal College, Nairobi, were offered at Form 4; more recently, Catholic boys could go to Strathmore—all these were more luxurious and exciting than school. It is self-evident that if one or more of the East African university colleges offered entry, or more Strathmores were built, or if more overseas scholarships at Form 4 were offered, it would become impossible to hold students in the school Sixth Forms—the comparisons would be too sharp and widespread. It was remarkable how at least some boys did in fact opt to remain at school (for example, at Budo College in Uganda) during the brief period when there was actually a choice between the school Sixth Form and the Makerere pre-university course; but this attitude could only be exceptional.

In summary, the case for the school Sixth Form is that it is economical, at a time when economy matters, as a means of catering for rapidly increasing numbers of entrants; that it has, and attracts, the right type of teacher for this stage of education, even if numbers or quality are hard to maintain; that it is in fact succeeding, and that arguments from age, largely a matter of comparison, are in any case weakening as ages fall, and ages will fall further if the primary course is reduced to seven or even six years.

But while there seems to be a strong case for the Sixth Form and Higher School Certificate course for an academic stream bound for university in East Africa or elsewhere, it does not follow that this should be the only method of continuing a fairly general education for a good slice of Fourth Form leavers. It is true that at present there are plenty of opportunities for vocational training for every student who passes School Certificate at all. But this will not always be the case; when the volume of School Certificate passes begins to rise more steeply, and the Africanisation programme is nearly complete, there may well be a 'surplus' of School Certificate holders in relation at least to formal opportunities for further education and training. The manpower estimates admit of this possibility, though only if economic growth remains at a low level right up to 1970. Moreover, whether justifiably or not, there is certain to be very strong political pressure from these Fourth Formers, via their parents, against accepting training from the Fourth Form level if by any means they can find entry to a university or college which will continue their general education further and enable them to enter forms of vocational training at a higher level and with greater prospects.

In fact, there will be a demand for a third choice, which is neither the Higher School Certificate course (with its wide academic syllabus) nor immediate training for teaching or agriculture or industry under the many departmental and industrial training schemes which have been mentioned.

In assessing this demand, it is important to distinguish between the current situation in East Africa and the situation which may arise by about 1966. At present, there is *an over-all shortage of good School Certificate passes*. If rather more of the 1963 or 1964 crop went straight to a university from Form 4 fewer would be available for the existing training schemes with Fourth Form entry, which are in many cases sadly short of suitable candidates already. In a word, the total supply of higher manpower is not increased by a single man, but rather more would become available after four years with a university Degree and rather less would enter the economy after two or three years of vocational training. If, indeed, Sixth Forms and the Higher School Certificate course were totally abolished, and university entry in East Africa were to be set at Form 4, with a four-year course, the supply of graduates would come after 4 years instead of 5 (2 in Higher School Certificate classes; 3 in university) but, again, the total supply would not be increased by a single man. Moreover, abolition would entirely cut off students from entry into United Kingdom universities.

However, looking further ahead, the case for a third choice becomes stronger. While, in my own view, it is vital to maintain a high standard of entry to the East African university and, by the same token, the right of entry to United Kingdom universities and a link with the best level in international scholarship, by 1965 or soon afterwards there may well be a group of Form 4 leavers, not wholly suited to Sixth Form work as at present defined, or to academic distinction, but still well suited to further general education before entering their life's vocation.

What form this extra outlet should take is still an open question. In the current situation there is much to be said, not for new institutions which could gain students by robbing existing training, but for up-grading some of the existing second level training schemes so that they offer better prestige and prospects. The training to agricultural diploma and to Medical Assistant, certain courses in technical colleges, certain types of Public Administration course, could all be raised in esteem by an overt association with the university, which could assist in staff and syllabus and examination, could sponsor the diploma, and could if necessary insist on a longer course, better equipment, etc. as the price of recognition. From such a policy now there could grow for the future Institutes of Technology, Colleges of Agricultural Technology, a Medical College, and other such institutions with a broad but practical course at 'diploma' level and, in suitable subjects, an opportunity for the best students to move sideways into a full university course with some credit for their attainment. Such a policy of building on the excellent foundation at second level would seem preferable to an attempt to found, very expensively, a whole range of 'Junior Colleges' or the like, and would avoid any danger of putting a foot down the slippery slope of reducing university standards. The case for 'Junior Colleges' or 'Liberal Arts Colleges' may arise more strongly in a few years' time.

(d) *No Places Available in a Special Subject*

This is a straightforward issue. The list on p. 51 outlines the main subjects—many more specialisms could be thought of and added —for which specific courses are not at present available in the public educational system or through specially provided courses. The list is certainly fairly long but much of it consists of specialized applications or branches of subjects which *are* in fact taught within the region—pharmacy, dentistry, mining engineering, electronics, stand out as subjects for which there might reasonably be a demand. It is, of course, clear that a developing country cannot possibly afford to provide the range of specialized education which a rich country can afford. There are therefore bound to be needs, in quite varied fields, for overseas education. Already the East African governments are asking for the provision of scholarships in subjects which are especially needed for their 'Africanisation' programmes. The main issue here lies between individual ambitions, which may be directed towards a course in sculpture or fashion designing, and public need.

(e) *The Paramount Value of Overseas Training*

Lastly, it can certainly be argued that, whether or no a particular form of education or training is available in East Africa, it is a good thing, perhaps even essential, that some young East Africans should go overseas, to widen horizons, to compare standards, to bring East Africa more firmly into the international society of educated and skilled people.

Clearly, there are valid reasons here. But in any case quite a large number of East Africans do go abroad, and must, for those subjects not available in East Africa; and in particular many go, and will continue to go, probably on an increasing scale, for post-graduate work in overseas universities. The real question at present is whether many should go, either at Form 4 or Form 6, even if a comparable training is in fact available locally, and even if they are required in subjects other than their first choice in the interests of national economic and social development.

It is not altogether useless to consider what happens in other more developed countries to achieve this real need for widening horizons. In Britain, the grammar school boy, and still more the university undergraduate, can and does spend vacations, at least occasionally, in European travel. Second, quite a few students, on completing a first Degree, go overseas for post-graduate work. Finally, many young entrants to industry and commerce are sent overseas to become familiar with some other allied branch of their business, after their initial training in Britain has been completed. There is little doubt about the value of all these experiences.

But the situation in Africa is rather different. Long distances and heavy expense make overseas vacations impossible for all but a negligible fraction of African students. Their position is perhaps nearer to that of the American student, who can travel 3,000 miles without leaving the United States. Even here, there is a vital difference. For, although the American student can find great variety in scene and manners, he travels always within a developed economy. The prime need of Africans is not so much to see other Africans states facing the same problems as his own, with the same levels of technology (though that itself is of value), but to see something utterly different: and this is hard to achieve without very long travel. In fact, many do not know their own country, save for their home area and the capital city; and there are values in internal travel both within East Africa and to neighbouring states. But travel to Europe, the USA or Russia adds an entirely new dimension.

Second, there are few outside organizations generously and even anxiously pressing offers of overseas scholarships on British or French or American boys. But in East Africa these offers are being made constantly, and they may not involve either the individual or his local government in any great expense. It might seem the greatest folly to inhibit in any way whatsoever the flow of Africans into the outer world, where they will gain, in certain ways, something which East Africa cannot give them.

There are local arguments in the opposite direction, partly the arguments of planners the world over, partly concerned with the the real effects of overseas experience on the individual. The planners naturally feel that an unregulated and unpredictable leakage of good material overseas, when training schemes at home are short of candidates, makes forward 'manpower' programmes impossible to fulfil. Moreover it disturbs the internal educational system, either by creaming off the best material and thereby lowering the standards and prestige of local institutions, or by offering the glittering prize of three years in the United States, Europe or Russia to the very boys who through lack of ability or character defects have failed to gain entry to East African schemes. And, indeed, it is established that possibly as many as forty first-class students refused places in East African colleges in 1962, in order to remain free and available for overseas scholarships. Further, governments intent upon rapid Africanisation are none too pleased to see potential District Commissioners or Agricultural Officers disappearing overseas to read irrelevant subjects, with the additional possibility that they will not be seen again in Africa for six years while they collect as many degrees and additional qualifications as they can afford and achieve. Some African governments are taking stern measures to prevent students going overseas for courses which are available at home.

Those concerned more with the effects on the individual would take a much less hostile view, and would use different criteria. They might well disagree with the planners' objections, arguing that plans are in any case always inaccurate or overtaken by events and that any individual who has had an enriching educational experience overseas, in no matter what subject, will in fact contribute something of special value to his home society on his return, possibly only in social and political ways, but possibly also in filling some economic gap not foreseen by the planners three or four years earlier. They would, however, distinguish sharply between the value of going overseas to an individual who is already fairly mature, stable in temperament and of good intelligence and the value of the same trip to those—and, alas, they have been numerous—who cannot adjust to new circumstances, who find themselves intellectually unable to achieve the award they sought, or who are driven towards neurotic breakdown by work, failure, lack of money, bad acquaintanceship, difficulties of language, climate, custom, sexual relationships, and much else. In this second view, suitability for overseas experience is far more a matter of personal qualities and attitudes than of fitting into the national plan.

There was, in 1962, a reasonable degree of agreement in East Africa about the value of overseas experience for African students and adults. Five years earlier many would have said the experience was frequently unsettling, resulting in the return to Africa of a young man either so attracted to Europe or America that he could not come to terms with his own people; or blinded by prejudice, as a result of unhappy personal experiences in his relations with Europeans either overseas or on return; or intolerably conceited and unwilling to accept a reasonable job of work. But today the African returning is sure of a job, is far less suspicious of Europeans because he feels that the anti-colonial struggle is won, and is therefore much more able to settle down quickly. Certainly, in 1962 the testimony in East Africa was almost unanimous—that a period overseas, even a short period of a few months, made a vast difference to self-confidence and breadth of vision. This was especially mentioned in relation to some older Africans, doing some fairly humble but valuable job—perhaps at a Farmers' Training Centre as an instructor. Just a few weeks seeing British or Dutch or American agriculture, a big city, Parliament, meeting a few practical farmers—this was enough to give reality and content to so many words and concepts, inevitably European, which he had heard, and used himself so often, in teaching African peasants more methodical farming or more efficient Co-operative methods. Moreover, it was a reward for years of honest work, probably worth more to him in prestige and in self-esteem than if the cost of his visit had been given as a salary increase spread over five years. It was emphasized, too, in relation to young trainees taking the diploma course in agriculture —a few months in America added enormously to their stature. It may well be today that it is the most able and brilliant Sixth Former, going to Harvard or Oxford, who may so flourish there that he gets out of tune with his own country and particularly with its political leaders, especially in the British (as against the French) context, where intellectuals and politicians are at opposite poles of thought and attitude.

SUMMARY

This discussion of the public case for overseas training, however inadequate, goes some way to identify certain classes of case where the expense and risk may be justified or necessary. It may be useful to make a somewhat bare list of these cases.

(a) Adults, who can go on a short course or visit both to up-grade some special training and to increase breadth and self-confidence.

(b) Young people who passed School Certificate recently, but fell off the educational ladder, for family or other personal reasons, and cannot get back onto it locally.

(c) Applicants for types of education or training (such as pharmacy) which is not available in East Africa but is of importance to the national effort.

(d) Trainees within government schemes for Africanisation who need particular experience, for example, range management of cattle, which may best be given overseas.

(e) Possibly those good Form 4 leavers who could benefit from a 'junior college' course, not available in East Africa. They would have to go to America, Canada, or to some country other than the UK, to get this particular experience.

(f) Form 4 leavers needing GCE(A) or technical college training which, mainly for geographical and similar reasons, they cannot get in East Africa.

(g) Graduates, for post-graduate specialization. To this list may well be added a last general class—young women requiring professional or semi-professional training not available in East Africa; and wanting also, and perhaps legitimately, a share in the contact with a sophisticated European world which their future husbands will often have had.

This list is rather narrowly circumscribed in recognition of the present situation in East Africa, which is one of shortage of candidates for existing higher educational and training schemes. There are some empty places in the university colleges, there is an acute shortage of good candidates for the higher levels of teacher training. But the arguments will begin to alter if, as is quite probable, the supply of good School Certificate passes expands so rapidly that this shortage is turned into a surplus. If the university maintains its entry qualifications, this is not likely to occur for long enough at Sixth Form level, provided the university is given necessary finance for expansion. But by 1965 or 1966 when the Africanisation programmes are near completion, there could develop a surplus of Form 4 leavers not immediately required for teacher training or other vocational schemes in their present form. If this should happen, with its accompanying political pressure from ambitious parents and Fourth Formers, expansion of some alternative facilities in East Africa might become urgent. The suggestion made here is that this would best be achieved by up-grading some of the vocational training to university diploma level rather than by creating new institutions or by increasing the volume of Fourth Formers going overseas.

CHAPTER VII

SCHOLARSHIP PROGRAMMES AND PROBLEMS

It was in the 1930s that the first trickle of Africans from East Africa began to go abroad for some form of higher education—the first recorded Kenya African to go was in 1930 from the Alliance High School on a scholarship to Fort Hare. Europeans and some of the richer Asians had, of course, sent their children to Britain (or sometimes to India; but Britain was often preferred by the Asians) for higher education, which was then not available in East Africa. There was a steady growth in this overseas movement on the Asian and European side, but only the occasional African went abroad in this pre-war period. Some of these, particularly from among the princely families in Uganda, went at their own expense. Jomo Kenyatta is notable among the earliest Kenyans to study in London.

After the war, when some Colonial Development & Welfare bursaries became available, and the British Council also increased its efforts, numbers began to rise much faster, with Kenya, the richest and most advanced, in the lead. By 1950, Kenya students abroad had risen to about 350, of whom 180 were supported by public funds; some Africans were in India with government of India scholarships, started in 1948. In the early 1950s the American government started to make awards; by 1955 there were over 900 Kenya students abroad, of whom 132 were Africans. Finally, in the last phase, many other governments entered the lists (Italy, Netherlands, Spain, Ethiopia, West Germany, UAR, Iron Curtain countries, Israel and the Commonwealth under various schemes). By 1960 the Kenya numbers were up to 2,500 and today (1963) the number may well be over 4,000 if private students are included. A similar pattern of growth, though on a smaller scale, took place in Tanganyika and Uganda, each of which had over 500 Africans and a somewhat higher number of Asians study-ing abroad in 1961–2. It is important to emphasize that the Asian contingent was always larger in the early years. The numbers in Britain from Kenya rose from 489 in 1959 to 764 in 1960 and to over 1,100 in 1962. Second, it is worth recording that African

G

university students in particular were not primarily concentrated in the UK at least since 1955. The Kenya figures for 1958–60 are:

Kenya African students in —	UK	India	Elsewhere
1958	74	70	75
1959	94	70	182
1960	126	103	537

The high figure for 'elsewhere' in 1960 means, in the main, the USA. There are now known to be over 1,000 African students from Kenya alone in the United States, the second highest figure for all overseas students there from a single country. Unfortunately, similar detail is not available for Uganda and Tanganyika for the earlier periods; but the pattern of growth was similar, slower in the early stages but catching up rapidly since 1956 or thereabouts.

The excitement and prestige of going overseas in the early days, above all for Africans, needs no emphasis. It has persisted, though now slightly dwindling, and is in itself a problem, as will appear.

Before, and just after, the War there was little problem of selection and control. Good offers of scholarships and bursaries were relatively few, and the government, the Missions and the British Council had little difficulty in seeing that they were taken up by the most deserving and eligible students, with only occasional exceptions. But from 1955 onwards, the situation began to get out of hand, particularly from the official standpoint. First, opportunities for higher education within East Africa began to grow fast. Second, the number of scholarships offered grew even faster and in a quite unco-ordinated way. Third, many Africans got hold of the UNESCO publication *Study Abroad*, which lists a great variety of scholarships and bursaries offered, and on their own initiative began to apply to a great variety of colleges, sometimes with success. Having gained an admission and perhaps enough money from private sources for the fare, with an undertaking (not always made good) of financial support from their family, they set off overseas and in many cases came to grief or spent years working in often poor jobs to pay for a long succession of courses, not always with ultimate success.

The result of this rapid growth of offers and of individual enterprise was to create a thoroughly disorderly situation. Headmasters complained that deserving boys were left out while far less able and less stable candidates landed scholarships. Africans went overseas for courses which were already available in East Africa; there was a danger that the East African university colleges would be starved of good entrants, because the best were being creamed off by overseas programmes. The East African governments were besieged with requests for financial help from students whom they would never have recommended to go overseas; yet they were embarrassed by accusations of imprisoning Africans at home when benevolent institutions and politically ambitious governments were offering them free education overseas. Finally, a small trickle of students, liable to increase to a flood, were smuggling themselves out of East Africa, without papers or money, to take up offers from Moscow and other Iron Curtain countries, on a network operating through Addis Ababa and Cairo. Much publicity was given to the confused state of affairs by the 'Mboya airlift', resulting from a grant to Mr Mboya of considerable funds from American sympathizers. The first contingent contained many Africans not well qualified for the kind of academic study for which they were destined in the United States, and there was a general, though slightly confused, feeling among Headmasters and officials that some kind of order must be restored. It is only fair to Mr Mboya to add that, for later contingents, he consulted carefully with the education authorities.

The impetus to gain some better control over this situation arose primarily from the 'Africanisation' programmes of the East African governments. As Departments began to draw up their schedules of possible replacements for the European expatriates who were leaving, it was clear that foreign scholarships were not being used purposively. Too few Africans were studying for the qualifications most urgently needed; too many were staying overseas, collecting degrees, when they were urgently needed at home; too many were getting qualifications, in the poorer American colleges or in India, which were not recognized as of adequate quality; too many were going overseas with inadequate qualifications; in some cases governments were faced with expensive repatriation, under international law, of students overseas who had become a charge on public funds, through failure in their courses, unemployment, physical or mental breakdown; the orderly direction of students to courses of education or training in East Africa was being upset by the siren voices from overseas; trainees, expensively brought to the starting post for productive work, were resigning their jobs, both in government and industry, to take up a tempting offer overseas—offers, it was felt, made not with the good of East Africa in mind, but to gain goodwill and gratitude from Africans for the donor government. Filling in application forms became an industry in the secondary schools, where the students' mail was (and still is) bespangled with the stamps and postmarks of half the States of America and half the capitals of Europe.

A second and supporting influence towards order came from the United States, where the universities and others by 1960 were becoming increasingly alarmed at the number of African students who were becoming destitute, failing in courses, embarrassing the colleges who had admitted them. Alarming estimates, as high as $2,000,000 were put forward as the cost of 'baling out' students from East Africa who had run into difficulties, either by enabling them to complete their courses or getting them home. To a smaller degree, educational and social institutions in Britain were feeling the same anxieties. A strong American delegation of College Presidents in 1960, followed by the Princeton Conference in 1961, went far to revise American policy.

As a result of these two convergent forces, a determined effort began to be made in all three countries to regain control and to use funds and men to the best advantage. This effort is still in its early stages, and by no means universally effective; but the real power behind it is the determination of East African governments to gain control of their manpower-planning, and a much more sober attitude in the United States towards the whole subject. It looks as if the government-to-government and the official agency programmes are already coming into reasonable shape; but there is still a considerable leakage, since Africans naturally continue to make direct applications if they can, and many well-meaning smaller institutions in the USA, and for that matter in the UK, continue to accept students without adequate enquiry as to their qualifications or probable financial support. As a single extreme instance—a Goan postal clerk who was offered, and took up, a place in an American college on the strength of a conversation in the Post Office with a visiting American governor of that particular institution.[1] The second volume of this Study, dealing with the UK situation, will describe some strange situations in some British institutions.[2]

Before dealing in detail with these arrangements for co-ordination, it may be useful to set out various ways in which applications or proposals for scholarships and bursaries may arise.

First, there are offers or programmes directly generated within East Africa. There may be East African government scholarships, won by competition, for study in overseas universities, usually in straightforward academic subjects. Some Missionary Societies also grant scholarships in this way from their own funds. The British Council has a limited number of three-month bursaries for UK visits (about eight per annum in each country). Here the student either wins his award by competition or is directly selected by the recommendation of responsible people. No trouble about co-ordination or quality arises.

---

[1] Who presumably thought she was helping an African.
[2] Notably the Balham & Tooting Technical College, the Colwyn Bay Wireless College, and the Bell Lane Institute.

Second, there are overseas study bursaries given through government departments for the Africanisation programme. Here, some assistance from outside countries may be involved. For example, American AID in 1962 was financing sixty 'Africanisation' awards for the Kenya government programme, in addition to another forty awards to enable students overseas to complete their courses. In some cases these arrangements are made by some direct contact between a Department in East Africa and an American college. For example, the University of West Virginia is taking Tanganyikan agricultural students for part of their diploma course, until the Morogoro College is in full operation; some Kenya agricultural diplomates are going for a ten-month course at Corvallis, Oregon, to return at the Degree level; some veterinaries, also from Kenya, are doing a year's study in Kansas to improve their qualifications; East African students have gone to Australia and New Zealand under similar schemes. Here again, selection of suitable candidates is in the hands of the relevant Department, and the only difficulty arises when a favoured candidate is lost to the Department's scheme because some other scholarship or opening looks more attractive to him.

Thirdly, the American programme deserves separate treatment, for its very size. Agencies and policies change very fast; but in 1962 the principal elements in American scholarship aid were as follows:

(a) *The AID programme*

Mainly centred on particular, and sometimes short, courses, often of a technical character, to complete a technical, professional or sub-professional qualification. Much AID effort has been closely correlated with Africanisation programmes, and many bursars are experienced adults.

(b) *USIS and other US Government Scholarships*

These are, in general, awards to younger students for pure academic work; they are admitted to places in US universities and technical institutes. The International Institute of Education (New York) administers some of the American government programmes.

(c) *ASPAU (African Scholarship Program of American Universities)*

This is a major scheme, initiated by the 'Ivy League' universities but including by 1962 no less than 192 universities and colleges in forty-one different American States. The programme has been supported by American Foundations and by the African-American Institute, which acts as the administrative agent in Africa and financial agent in the United States. Major support to the programme is also given by

AID, and in effect the amount of AID funds allocated virtually decrees the number of students which ASPAU can accept. In the 1962 programme about 450 places in the associated colleges could have been available but AID support was limited to 300. This figure covers the programmes for East, Central, West and Southern Africa (the High Commission Territories), the ex-Belgian Congo, and Ethiopia. Students can make direct application to the ASPAU representative, and are required to have either HSC, SC Division I or high Division II passes; they must not be enrolled in any other college or institution unless the prescribed course there finishes in the year of the application. The large number of applications (2,700 from East, Central and Southern Africa in 1961) is reduced to more manageable numbers by a standard Preliminary Scholastic Aptitude Test, and the remainder are given personal interview. There is now close co-operation and co-ordination between the ASPAU operation and the local African governments. The pilot project, under which twenty-four students went to America in the autumn of 1960, was outstandingly successful, judged by the excellent academic reports on the students' work in their American colleges. The 1962 programme offered places to about 150 students from East, Central or Southern Africa.

Next, the large number of scholarships offered by other external governments to Africa must be mentioned. These differ both in size, quality and purpose. At one end might be placed long-established schemes, such as that of the government of India for African students, administered through recognized local committees, and having no more marked political content than a general gesture of goodwill between two Commonwealth governments. At the other extreme might be put sudden offers of scholarships (sometimes in large numbers), such as that made by UAR to Tanganyika in 1962 for forty Tanganyika students; or the offers of scholarships, in Peking or Poland or the Patrice Lumumba University in Moscow, which itinerant and ambitious African politicians are apt to bring back from their travels, and which are designed both to increase the popularity of the politician and to indoctrinate some of the young generation of Africans with what he feels to be appropriate ideas and ideals. These were seldom co-ordinated with the Education Departments, but were more apt to be handed out as largesse by the possessor to supporters or potential supporters in his own country. It is difficult to keep track of these, since in some cases they are handled in a purely personal way, though in others harassed education officials are told to produce suitably qualified applicants —which at present is not always easy. Between these two extremes lie a number of scholarship offers from foreign governments (in Western Europe, North Africa, Israel, West Africa, and elsewhere) which are newcomers to the scene but normally make reasonable arrangements for administration.

The UK programme, which in total numbers is certainly the largest, is far more difficult to describe concisely, for it is by far the most varied. It may originate in scholarships or bursaries financed by local governments, by offers from the British government through the Department of Technical Co-operation; in arrangements made directly, or through the British Council, by the Colonial Office or CRO: by Missions and other voluntary organizations and charitable Trusts; through the larger British or East African employers (such as East African Railways & Harbours). It may be at university level for a Degree course, in technical colleges, agricultural colleges, the Royal School of Mines, Loughborough, and many other institutions; and it may consist in short specially sponsored visits and attachments, for the study of local government, diplomatic practice, taxation, national health insurance or a host of other social and administrative techniques. The detail of these UK students will be dealt with in the second volume of this Study. The publicity given to American and other foreign programmes sometimes obscures the constant flow of students and adults to Britain, which has been easily and unobtrusively arranged owing to the close personal links between the expatriate civil servants, business men and Missions and their home country. As Africanisation proceeds faster, some of these links will be broken.

Lastly, there is the 'private' programme—that is, the flow of students who gain admission to some overseas institution by their own efforts, often raise money for the fare from their family, and hope to support themselves by part-time and vacation work during their overseas study. It has always been extremely difficult to keep any accurate figures of this private movement. Passport control figures are of limited use, particularly since the prospective student may change his mind and his course of study when he arrives at his destination. It is futile to hope that accurate figures, showing country of origin and course followed, could be obtained from the score or more countries to which East Africans may go. In consequence, the stream cannot easily be measured at either end. The new arrangements for co-ordination and control may make it more possible to keep track of outgoing students at the East African end, with at least details of country of destination and course to be followed at some particular institution within it.

Scholarship and bursary applications are not, of course, confined to applications for a first grant. Out of about 120 sieved applicants for Kenya government bursaries in 1962, over fifty were already following courses overseas (about thirty of these in the USA) and were needing further help to continue or complete their course. In some cases their programmes were not altogether modest—one proposed to tackle a BSc., MSc., and Ph.D. in America, starting from School Certificate—possibly a nine-year programme, started by a one-year bursary from his local African District Council. A large number of applicants had already obtained admission to particular British or American institutions, and were next looking round for some source of finance. It is evident that a great deal of paper work, both by applicants and the donors of bursaries, is caused by the common pattern of giving a student a one-year grant, although he is known to be starting a three-year course. Moreover, the constant state of anxiety which the student must feel, each year, as he tries to provide for the remainder of his course, must be very bad for his academic work. The ASPAU programme is based on grants to see the student right through his course, with firmer guarantees of his own contribution, and this is surely a great improvement. The old system was that a student who could show an admission to a college overseas (and, in America, it did not have to be an 'accredited' college), *plus* $450 for his fare, could virtually claim an exit permit as of right. Much stricter conditions may well be demanded in future.

It may be of interest to illustrate, for a single country, the range and variety of scholarship and bursary provision. Appendix II reproduces a note prepared in Kenya (1962) of the main schemes; and even this does not include a great variety of private donors, the African District Council bursaries, offers from individual American colleges, and many other miscellaneous possibilities which a per-severing African student in search of financial aid could discover.

The procedure for co-ordination, established in Kenya and Tanganyika, and with less rigidity in Uganda (although Uganda was the first to establish a central co-ordinating committee in the mid-1950s) consists basically of a central co-ordinating committee, to which all, or at least as many as possible, scholarship proposals by donors will be submitted. It is some evidence of the seriousness with which this subject is now regarded that this machinery has been established at Cabinet level in Tanganyika and by direction of the Council of Ministers in Kenya. The 'teeth' of these committees really lie in their close relations with the Passport control; if need be, a student proposing to set off overseas could find himself refused an exit permit unless his proposed excursion carried the central committee's approval. The Kenya committee, established in the late summer of 1962, has an African Chairman (the Speaker of the House, as a neutral) and includes representatives of the Education Department and of the main Missions. Donor countries are represented on the Committee when their scholarships are on the agenda. In addition, each major scholarship scheme has its own local selection committee, upon which the Kenya government is always represented. The role of the central committee (KOSAC—Kenya Overseas Scholarship Advisory Committee) was tentatively defined to include—(a) offering advice to potential scholarship donors on the form in which an offer would be most useful and acceptable; (b) if requested, selecting or helping to select students; (c) checking lists of students proposed by the donor; (d) approving scholarships or bursaries obtained by private effort by students; (e) maintaining a register of scholarship applicants. The committee has terms of reference which emphasize its duty to take only educational, and not political, considerations into account in making its recommendations.

At the time of this investigation, the committee had only just been established, and it is too early to say how well it will work or what difficulties it may meet. Clearly, no colonial administration, in the present era, could have established such a body without bitter opposition. The intention to control 'private' students through the passport procedure is a drastic step—it may be only gently administered—which shows how firmly public need is to be preferred by African governments to private ambitions. Yet in the long run governments will have to pay more attention to the incentives and rewards of various careers; for although it may be possible to control scholarships and initial training, it is not possible to hold men indefinitely in jobs, however great their national importance, where pay and prospects compare too badly with other opportunities. This is a lesson learned in West Africa from the difficulties of enforcing the bonding system. Manpower policy must be accompanied by a wage, salary and career policy which at least does not conflict too strongly and if possible pulls in the same direction. This question of individual motive is considered in the next chapter.

It remains to consider briefly the probable future trend of overseas education and training in East Africa. At the beginning of 1963 Tanganyika and Uganda had each probably about 1,500 Africans and Asians studying overseas, Kenya perhaps twice that number.[1] Of this fairly large number, rather less than a third might be on a full three or four-year course; the majority would be abroad for about a year or two years to obtain a particular qualification or experience; and, at least in future, a good proportion of these will be sent by governments as part of Africanisation programmes. Very roughly, if 800 students from any one country went overseas each year, with 400 returning after the first year, 200 after the second and 100 after each of the third and fourth years, there would be a constant figure of 1,500 students overseas in any year. As this may be a confusing calculation, Table A shows how this works.

[1] See chapters IV & V.

TABLE A

Outflow of Students		Return Flow of Students				Total Students Abroad	
Year	Number	From Year 1	From Year 2	From Year 3	From Year 4	Number	Year
1	800					800	1
2	800	400				1,200	2
3	800	200	400			1,400	3
4	800	100	200	400		1,500	4
5	800	100	100	200	400	1,500	5

4,000 in   800   1,500 remains
5 years   returned   constant
       from Year 1

Note: The supply of returning students to the economy would thus be in the fifth and subsequent years:

University Graduates   100 from a 4-year course (From Year 1)
                             100 from a 3-year course (From Year 2)

                            200

2-year trained   200 from a 2-year course (From Year 3)
1-year trained   400 from a 1-year course (From Year 4)

Grand Total   800

An alternative distribution of students, with a higher proportion of graduate course and fewer on 2-year courses might be (from 800) 400 on 1-year course, 100 on 2-year course, 200 on 3-year university course, 100 on 4-year university course. This would give 1,600 abroad at any time, and a return flow, in Year 5 and subsequently of:

University Graduates   300   (100 from Year 1, 200 from Year 2)
2-year Course   100   (From Year 3)
1-year Course   400   (From Year 4)

                           800

One thousand six hundred sent yearly, in the same proportions, would maintain 3,000 abroad. If about 400 of this 1,600 were taking first Degrees, of three or four years, from each country, this would give a supply of about 1,200 graduates per annum for East Africa, against a supply of perhaps 750–1,000 from East African university colleges under their probable programmes. It would seem, from the man-power estimates, although these are conservative, that a supply of this size might even outrun at least the essential requirements, and would mean a heavy drain on the output from secondary schools; for over a five-year period it would involve sending 1,600 a year, i.e. 8,000 students from each country from a *total* estimated School Certificate output of:[1]

	1961–66	1966–71
Kenya	14,550	26,000
Uganda	7,500	11,500
Tanganyika	10,500	16,000

[1] See chapter III.

Although, for the time being, some of those going abroad will be adults on up-grading courses, in the longer run the numbers going overseas must be closely related to the secondary output. It is highly unlikely that either Uganda or Tanganyika would wish or need to send so high a proportion of their secondary output overseas in the second five-year period, when far more training facilities will be available in East Africa. It would therefore seem probable that the present demand represents a peak load, and that the probable outflow of students from East Africa will settle down at about 600 per annum for Uganda, perhaps 750 for Tanganyika, and around 1,000 for Kenya. This would give respectively 1,200, 1,450 and 2,000 students overseas at any one time.

As regards the type of course which these students will seek, it seems likely that numbers going abroad for a Degree course post-HSC will dwindle to almost nothing for a few years—the East African University can take them. Post-graduate specialization should rise. But the largest numbers are likely to come at the School Certificate level, and for one-year courses for adult trainees in government service and Public Utilities. The School Certificate boys will fall into two groups—those wishing to take GCE(A) and a special technical training; and those wishing a four-year American-type college course. This would argue that the main *British* problem of looking after students will lie in the technical colleges (post-graduate students should not cause much trouble) while the American problem will lie in the first year or two of the four-year college course. In both cases the growing co-ordination and control at the African end should make things much easier.

Clearly, as general policy, it will be far better when the day is reached when Africans do not go overseas for training until they are much more mature than many are at present—at the post-graduate or higher technical level. The question which requires a policy answer quite soon is the right treatment for those who will never reach high technical or academic standards and who get only whatever post-primary 'modern' education Africa can afford; and this will have to be decided in Africa.

BURSARIES, SCHOLARSHIPS AND LOANS FOR HIGHER EDUCATION

For information and general guidance a note on the various forms of aid for education beyond Cambridge School Certificate is appended below.

A. AID FROM KENYA GOVERNMENT FUNDS

1. *Kenya Government Bursaries* (*Overseas*)

(a) Open to all races subject to the following conditions:
   (i) Student must be over sixteen years old;
   (ii) Student must have been at a Kenya school or schools for a minimum of five years;
   (iii) Parent or guardian must have resided in Kenya for a minimum of five years;
   (iv) Student must have been admitted or have received promise of admission to an institution of higher learning overseas.

(b) African and Arab students receive awards on the 'all expenses paid' basis. This includes passages, fees, maintenance, necessary text books and equipment, warm clothing allowance and, where necessary, dependants' allowances. Arabs studying at Beit-el-Ras are eligible.

(c) European, Asian and Goan students receive partial assistance only.

(d) Awards are not usually made for courses equally available in East Africa. Preference is given for courses likely to be useful in the development of Kenya.

(e) Africans and Arabs have to sign an undertaking to serve the Kenya government for a minimum of three years on return. Europeans, Asians and Goans sign no such undertaking, but preference in awards is given to those likely to return and work in Kenya.

(f) Applications are made on dates advertised in the public press to the Director of Education. Government servants apply through their departments.

2. *Kenya Open Scholarship*
   (a) Multi-racial.
   (b) Automatic award to the Kenya student who passes with the highest marks in Cambridge Oversea Higher Certificate from a Kenya school. The name is communicated to the Director of Education by the Cambridge Local Examinations Syndicate annually.
   (c) One scholarship of £100 per annum awarded each year. It may be held in addition to a bursary or loan.

3. *Kenya Government Bursaries to Makerere*
   (a) Multi-racial.
   (b) Subject to admission to Makerere being confirmed.
   (c) Amount varies with financial situation of family, but can be up to full costs including pocket-money if necessary.
   (d) Applications to be made to the Director of Education.

4. *Kenya Government Bursaries to the Royal Technical College, Nairobi*
   (a) Multi-racial.
   (b) Subject to admission to the Royal Technical College being confirmed.
   (c) Amount varies with financial situation of family but can be up to full costs including pocket-money, clothing etc. where necessary.
   (d) Applications to be made to the Director of Education.

5. *Teachers' Scholarships*
   (a) Multi-racial.
   (b) Open to:
       (i) Serving teachers in government or aided schools.
       (ii) Trainees in training colleges.
       (iii) Higher Certificate candidates in local high schools who have given an undertaking to teach.
   (c) Europeans receive partial cost of course—£250 per annum on undertaking to teach in a Kenya government school for a number of years equal to the number of years for which scholarship is drawn.
   (d) Asians receive a full award including dependants' allowance if required and are bound to teach for at least three years on return. Government servants are placed on leave without pay 'in the interests of public service'.
   (e) Applications are called for annually through Provincial Education Officers and heads of schools.
   (f) Scholars are selected by departmental selection boards with due consideration to the needs of the service.

(g) Normally applicants must be under twenty-five years of age, exceptionally up to thirty years of age.

6. *Bursaries for Teachers in Training*

These are for trainees in local Asian teacher training colleges and applications have to be made to the Director of Education.

7. *Higher Education Loans*

(a) Applications are received annually from parents or guardians of all races.

(b) Students must have been admitted or received promise of admission to an institution of higher learning and must be not less than seventeen years old.

(c) Parents or guardians must be permanent residents of Kenya.

(d) Loans are advanced subject to the following conditions:

    (i) Security in the form of title deeds, insurance policies or personal bonds must be provided.

    (ii) Loans are advanced in half-yearly instalments and interest at the rate of £4¾ per cent per annum is paid in half-yearly instalments in arrear.

    (iii) There is a moratorium of at least one year after the completion of the student's course after which the loan with interest at £4¾ per cent has to be repaid in sixteen equated half-yearly instalments of principal and interest over a period of eight years.

B. NOT FROM KENYA GOVERNMENT FUNDS

1. *Government of India Scholarships*

(a) Africans and Arabs only eligible.

(b) School Certificate with four credits required—degree course offered.

(c) Applications to Commissioner for India in East Africa on dates advertised annually.

(d) Eight each year.

(e) Amount of Rs. 200 per month for maintenance in a hostel.

(f) No passages or dependants' allowances.

2. *Government of Pakistan Scholarships*

Same as government of India but usually two each year (though five in 1962).

3. *United States Scholarships*

   (a) Multi-racial.

   (b) Graduate or London Intermediate standard required.

   (c) Full costs given but scholarship only for one year normally.

   (d) No dependants' allowances.

   (e) Application to USIS annually on dates advertised.

4. *Rattansi Trust Bursaries*

   (a) Multi-racial—income is divided into five equal parts for Europeans, Africans, Muslims, non-Muslims and Ismailis.

   (b) Up to £300 plus travel expenses if required.

   (c) Seven years residence of parents or guardians and seven years Kenya schooling of student required.

   (d) School Certificate is minimum qualification.

   (e) Student must have been admitted or received promise of admission to an institute of higher learning overseas.

   (f) Applications to the Secretary, Rattansi Charitable Trust, PO Box 111, Nairobi.

5. *Gandhi Memorial Trust*

Bursaries to Royal Technical College. Application to the Secretary of the Trust.

6. *EAR & H Bursaries*

Bursaries of £450 per annum to the United Kingdom universities for Degree studies. Two per year. Multi-racial. Applications invited by notice in public press to be sent to General Manager EAR & H, Nairobi.

7. *Dan Pienaar Memorial Fund*

European only. British subject born and permanently resident in East Africa for studies in South African universities.

8. *Government of Italy Scholarships*

These awards are available only for East Africa. They cover the cost of full maintenance and tuition fees and where necessary all travel expenses. The awards are for both undergraduate and post-graduate studies. Applications are made to the Italian Consul General, Nairobi, on dates which he advertises in the daily press.

9. *Government of Ethiopia Scholarships*

Eight scholarships are awarded annually, providing the cost of full maintenance and tuition fees and where necessary, of passages. The awards are for undergraduate studies in Ethiopia.

Applications are made to the Ethiopian Consul General, Nairobi, on dates which he advertises in the daily press.

10. *Kenya Farmers' Association Bursaries*

Bursaries to children of European farmers for studies overseas.

11. *Commonwealth Scholarship Plan*

A number of scholarships are awarded annually under this scheme in United Kingdom, Canada, New Zealand, Australia, Ceylon, India, Rhodesia and Nyasaland, Malta and Malaya; other Commonwealth countries may also eventually offer such scholarships.

The awards include the cost of passages, tuition and maintenance, and are mainly for post-graduate studies, although awards may occasionally be made for courses at the intermediate level.

Teacher training scholarships in United Kingdom and Australia are also awarded under a connected scheme, covering the cost of tuition and *minimum maintenance* only. Candidates will be selected through Ministry of Education channels.

Applications are made to the Permanent Secretary, on dates advertised in the daily press.

12. A number of private Asian donors of scholarships to India and Pakistan have been excluded from review; scholarships offered by colleges in America; and other private donors; as the number, amount and so on, is irregular and there is no clear information about them.

CHAPTER VIII

PRIVATE AMBITIONS AND INCENTIVES

During the long period when training and educational opportunities in East Africa were very limited (as was the supply of fully qualified African students) the habit of snatching eagerly at any chance of going overseas, however imperfectly financed, naturally grew up. The resulting prestige was great, and often lead to a career which took a man far out ahead of his contemporaries, either in salaried work or in political leadership. A period even in the poorest American college or Indian university had this effect, and seemed infinitely desirable. As education grew in East Africa, the best students, who had the entry to Makerere, probably became more wary of poor quality qualifications, though no less anxious for overseas study; in consequence, the furious pursuit of bursaries and scholarships moved downwards a little, to those who had not quite achieved success in East Africa, saw no hope of further education there, and realized that their last chance lay overseas. This process has continued. There were in 1962 at least some Africans who preferred to go to Sixth Form work and an East African university college, with its 'guaranteed' quality of degree and the certainty of recognition and employment, to any but the most enticing and cast-iron overseas offer. Even after HSC a few still preferred Makerere to all but the best American and British universities. But at a lower level, among those with a Division II or III SC pass, with GCE only, or with a failure in HSC, the attraction of overseas study was and is as great as ever. Only one danger now begins to loom up—that while the student is abroad the best jobs and openings in East Africa will be filled. This certainly gives pause to some students, who have no wish to find on return all governmnet posts filled with young men and promotion prospects non-existent.

It is not accusing Africans of lack of patriotism to say that their choice of action now is the subject of anxious personal calculation in which public need plays little part. For one thing almost any further education or training will serve some public need: who would become a humble schoolteacher when far better pay and prospects may lie elsewhere, without great extra personal effort or family expense? The elements which enter into this calculation (the same for most young men and women anywhere in the world) are fairly complex. A job now, with some pay, or a better job later after more education? The family will have some say in this. Prestige? Salary? Promotion prospects? The excitement of going abroad? Getting out of school into the adult world? Personal vocation, aptitude or preference? All these factors must be weighed, and the weights differ from year to year with the changing situation. If we take first the African boy or girl who has just taken School Certificate, the range of choice is fairly wide. If he or she has a good pass, in Division I or high in Division II, there will be open:

(a) Sixth Form in East Africa.
(b) Possibly a scholarship to a good American or other (not UK) college.
(c) Government training to 'diploma' level—agriculture, medical services, etc.
(d) Apprenticeship in a large firm or Public Utility.
(e) A GCE(A) course at a technical institute, or possibly at Royal College, leading to a technical and possibly professional qualification.
(f) Teacher training at the KTI (Grade A) level.

It is probable that, in 1962, opportunities were ranked by most African boys in roughly that order, although the American programme would have come first for many. It is, perhaps, surprising that it did not come first for all. But an American place is more of a risk. It is necessary to refuse a place in East Africa before the candidate is considered for the ASPAU programme, so that he is taking a risk of falling between two stools. Not everyone wants to go abroad for four years; and Africans are aware that not all American Degrees are at present acceptable in East Africa. In contrast, the progression within East Africa is assured, and a job is assured at the end of it. Government training also comes high on the list, because it leads straight to an appointment as, for example, Assistant Agricultural Officer, with a scale starting at over £650 (compared to £320 for a KTI teacher) and rising to £1,100. Moreover, these field staff have at least a hope of making the top grade, Agricultural Officer, by promotion after experience. The same applies to at least the Tanganyika medical scheme, and possibly to the training schemes for central administration. Pay in large industry will also be good, but promotion prospects perhaps more distant and subject to a stringent efficiency test. The Polytechnic or technical institute is far less glamorous than a university, and the possibilities of rising by that route to professional level are probably not fully understood. Teaching (in the top forms of primary, or at best the lower forms of secondary) comes a bad last in pay and prospects.

For those with poor passes, the Sixth Form is unobtainable, and therefore an overseas scholarship far more attractive. Government training will probably only lead to the third level of extension work or clerical grades centrally. Thus, failing a scholarship overseas, industry becomes more attractive, and teaching more acceptable for those who want security and have some vocation. For the failures, industry, teaching, government clerical training, if it can be had, or possibly a correspondence course to complete at least GCE (O) followed by a GCE(A) course in East Africa or abroad may be the only choices.

At the higher level of HSC, those who pass have a university entrance at command, and the only question is whether to take it in Africa or aim at an overseas course. Very few indeed would step outside the academic stream at this point, save possibly girls for marriage or family reasons and a few boys who may be attracted either into an industrial firm by a promise of management training which is likely to include an overseas course, or into one of the new teacher training schemes with entry at HSC leading to a diploma and a high degree of security and professional interest as a quite senior secondary school master. Those who fail may also be able to enter the teacher training course; otherwise, they would still be available for a scholarship programme or for quite good opportunities in industry or government.

It is scarcely necessary to analyse the choices open to African university graduates—the world is at their feet. Up to 1963 at least, government employment will look most attractive because promotion can be so rapid as senior expatriates leave. Thereafter, as the government service fills up, industry or graduate teaching may get a better supply of recruits. To a few, who are set upon an academic career, post-graduate work overseas will have high attractions; this will also apply to those who want to establish themselves in one of the scarcer, more specialized skills not taught in East Africa.

As an illustration of these choices, we obtained a detailed breakdown of the choices made by boys at Tabora government secondary school in 1961–62. Out of 60 boys (a double stream) leaving Form 4:

18 went to Form 5 (2 of these were short listed for America, failed, and got back into a Form 5, one at Tabora, one at Munali (N. Rhodesia))
2 were offered places in USA or New Zealand
1 went to Sandhurst
11 went into government, of whom
2 to agricultural training (prospects to diploma level)
2 to Police
2 to Game Departments

2 to Medical Department (prospects
of course for Rural Medical Practitioner)
2 to Co-operative Development Dept.
1 to Interpreter (High Court)

9 went to teacher training
9 went to Williamsons Diamond Mine (of whom 2 sent to Dar-
es-Salaam Technical Institute full
time)
2 went to East African Railways & Harbours
1 went to a bank
1 to an accountant's job
6 unknown
_____
60

Grouping these choices even further, the result is,

Form 5 or overseas scholarship	21 (=one-third)
Industry, Commerce, Railways	13
Government	11
Teacher Training	9
Unknown	6
	—
	60

A similar analysis of Sixth Form career choices at the same school
is as follows:

To Makerere	14	(6 Arts, 3 teacher training, 3 medicine, 2 veterinary)
To Dar-es-Salaam	5	(law)
To Royal College	1	(engineering Higher Certificate with EAR & H)
To USA	3	
To Denmark	3	(veterinary science)
	—	
Total University	26	(= nearly two-thirds)
	—	
To Government	3	(Geological Survey, Co-operative Department, agriculture)
Commerce & Industry	11	(railways 4, Williamsons 3 (1 to Camborne), accountants 2, bank 1, Agip (in Italy) 1)
Broadcasting	1	(TBC)
	—	
	41	

Probably two-thirds, and possibly three-quarters, of those going to a university will come back to jobs in government.

A very similar pattern exists in other schools, although in some cases it is a bank, sometimes a particular firm, sometimes the Railways, sometimes the Post Office which seem to have a particular link with a particular school, and attract exceptional numbers of applicants. There are, of course, exceptional cases. For example, the government secondary school at Bwira (Mwanza, Tanganyika) had not produced a single candidate for teacher training in four batches of School Certificate passes; whereas at least two Uganda schools (Nabumali, near Mbale, and Tororo) described teacher training as easily a first priority choice. Both these are Mission schools, and quite probably generate a vocation for teaching among their pupils; moreover, the range of opportunity outside teaching in Uganda is smaller.

For African girls, opportunities are more limited, and further artificially limited by the ignorance of some school staffs as to the opportunities which in fact exist. We were informed more than once that nursing, teaching and domestic science were the only opportunities for girls—which was, of course, almost true up to about 1955. In fact, a considerably wider range of opportunity is now opening for girls with School Certificate or better, partly in government offices and partly in industry and commerce. We were lucky to obtain a complete 'career record' of the girls from Gayaza High School (Buganda) as follows:

Stage I (before the girls took the Cambridge Overseas School Certificate)

During this period, of those leaving school 76 trained as primary teachers, 62 took up nursing, 14 joined the Social Welfare Department.

Stage II 1952—December 1961

During this period a certain number of girls left before completing the Cambridge Overseas School Certificate and mostly entered, as previously, the junior grades of the nursing and teaching professions.

Cambridge School Certificate:

Total number of candidates entered 140
Total number of passes 138, as follows: Grade I   54
                                               Grade II 66
                                               Grade III 13
(introduced 1959)   GCE only 5

Of these:

37 were accepted into the University College at Makerere (2 into the Faculty of Science, 25 into the Faculty of Arts and 10 into the School of Fine Art)

6 were accepted into the Royal Technical College, Nairobi.

28 joined Higher School Certificate (Advanced Level) classes in other schools (opened 1959) and Gayaza (1962)

24 proceeded to the Junior Secondary Teacher Training College at Buloba while 2 are at teacher training colleges in England, one in the USA

21 took up nursing (of whom 8 are completing the SRN England)

4 took up physiotherapy (of whom 2 are now studying in Liverpool and 1 in Bristol). The other qualified in Bristol

2 did clerical training

1 entered the Department of Social Welfare and another joined the Agricultural Institute

1 has gained a teaching diploma in domestic science in Bath

1 after finishing the Advanced Level at Sherborne School is now reading History at Girton College, Cambridge.

Old girls of all decades have played and are playing an exceedingly important part in the development of the country.

Of the total number of eleven women graduates in the country, eight are Gayaza old girls. An old girl is the only African woman member of the National Assembly, and the first woman parliamentary secretary. Another old girl is a representative on the Central EA Assembly. Others are leading members concerned with the organization of such bodies as the YWCA, the Uganda Teachers' Association, the Mothers' Union and the Girl Guide Association, and many are wives of chiefs and leading professional men.

For Asians, the limitation of choice is partly voluntary, partly imposed. Few, if any, opportunities exist in agriculture in East Africa, except on the large Asian sugar estates. Engineering and medicine attract by far the greatest number, no doubt partly because a good qualification in either has an international currency. At the lower levels, technical training in building and mechanical engineering, training in accountancy and book-keeping, and 'apprenticeship' in a family business are the natural outlets. We were told on several occasions that Asians with any financial resources liked, if possible, to take a GCE(A) level in Britain—which they achieve in one year—and go on to medical training there. Law is another profession attractive to Asians; it is doubtful how many Asians the Dar-es-Salaam law school will admit, since the Tanganyika Government will certainly wish to give preference to Africans.

The Asian community as a whole is dangerously vulnerable in East Africa, and there is little question of conflict between individual choice and public need: Asians are only anxious to find a form of training in which they will have an opportunity to earn a living. The conflict here is within public policy—for all three East African states are desperately short of locally trained engineers, doctors, lawyers, pharmacists, technicians; but all three are reluctant to offer posts, through any official channel, to Asians: in many cases they would prefer that a European expatriate should keep the job warm for an African later on, since the European can be conveniently removed and compensated at the right moment. Indeed, even commercial firms and Public Utilities, anxious to please African opinion, are cutting down or actually stopping all Asian recruitment for this reason. The motives are understandable; but the plain fact is that a great waste of potential skill and contribution to the East African economy is at present going on, through deliberate government policy, and this must modify the sympathy for African demands for massive educational aid, scholarships and subsidized places in Western institutions. It was distressing to find that Asian fathers, who had given twenty years' service to an East African government or a Public Utility, were unable to place fully qualified sons in the same service, not through shortage of jobs or excess of qualified applicants, but on purely racial grounds—the candidates were not even called for interview, on the admission of the employer.

In attempting any more general estimate of the degree to which there is correspondence between public need and at least those elements of private incentive which can be affected by public policy, it is necessary to remember that East Africa is in an emergency situation, and in a process of fast economic and social change. The spread of rewards between the African peasant, or even the paid labourer, at one end and the senior salaried official at the other is enormous. The labourer's rate is from £7 to £8 per month—say £80 per annum, and this is a consolidated rate including cost-of-living allowance, housing allowance, and ration allowance (or value of food provided).[1] For artisans, where there is a considerable range, pay might be from £15 to £20 or even £25 per month (£180–£240 per year). At the other end of the scale, the senior civil servant may draw £2,500 per annum—25 times the labourer's wage and 10 or 12 times the artisan's. In consequence, there is bound to be a zone in the middle ranges where very great differences in salary and prospects hang on small differences in qualifications. A primary education, followed by two years at a trade school, may bring an African to artisan level. A secondary education and School

[1] Federation of Kenya Employers, Nairobi 1961, rates for unskilled adult labour.

Certificate puts him in line for an American scholarship or at least diploma training. Thus entry to a secondary school and School Certificate itself makes a vast financial difference to a boy's prospects.

Further, as the entry point for some of the lower grades of training, such as third level field workers, is raised to School Certificate, while entry to diploma level training is also at that level, the School Certificate holders themselves are divided sharply. The top third will move towards a university degree and a starting salary of up to £1,000 in their job; the next third may reach diploma level training, leading to a starting salary of £500–£700; the last third will be at £300 a year level, possibly as teachers. This emphasis not merely on the SC examination, but on the exact performance in it, puts the most frightening emphasis on cramming, and is the despair of school masters. It may be that at a later stage entry to diploma level training will be raised to include those who have done *some* Fifth or Sixth Form work, though not the full HSC course. This would divide the levels of entry to careers more clearly.

The great span of differentials also makes it extremely difficult to find the right level for teachers. In all underdeveloped countries the ratio of the simplest primary teacher's earnings to that of the illiterate mass is far higher than in rich economies—possibly a factor of 4 to 1 instead of 2 to 1 or less. He is on the first critical step out of unskilled labour. But there is equally a vast difference between him and the fully Westernized official. The difficult man to place is the senior primary or junior secondary teacher (SC plus two years training). To put him even in the lower ranks of the 'upper' class— say at £500 or £600 a year starting salary—is enormously expensive; to leave him where he is today—at the level of a senior artisan on £320—is to lose all good quality recruits. At the Siriba (Kenya) Teacher Training College it was possible in 1958 and 1959 to select 60 applicants for KTI training all with good SC passes; in 1960, the quality fell; in 1961 three-quarters of an intake of 60 were SC *failures;* in 1962 only 40 entrants could be found (20 of the 60 accepted did not report for the course) and almost all were SC failures. At the Kagumo Teacher Training College (Kenya), 50 per cent of the 1962 intake were SC failures.

An implication of this situation is that at present an African society is being built up with far too wide a gap between top and bottom, partly because the top scales of pay have been related to those paid to expatriates from a society with more than ten times the national income per head, while the bottom scales are still related to a peasant standard of life. School Certificate separates the sheep from the goats; hence its enormous importance. For the scholarship donors the implication may be gradually to up-grade the qualifications needed for overseas awards—for the Division II or III SC holder ought to be filling the middle salary grades, and the Division I going on to Sixth Form work before considering a university. As the volume of Africans in secondary education begins to swell, this more selective use of overseas scholarships and bursaries may be easier to establish and administer. In the long run, when SC comes to be taken at the age of about sixteen or seventeen, probably very few indeed should go straight overseas at that age and level, most first Degrees should be taken in East Africa, and overseas scholarships should be mainly concentrated on post-graduate work and on technical or technological specialization.

CHAPTER IX

CONCLUSIONS—SOME POLICY ISSUES

This appraisal of educational opportunity in East Africa has been written in a somewhat cold-hearted way. It is sensible to look first at the facts and figures, the arguments for economy and efficiency, the need for controls to avoid waste, inequity and disappointment. But it is also quite wrong to neglect or belittle the large element of feeling which enters into this situation, both at the political level and for individuals, and particularly wrong for Africa, where feeling runs high. Politically, African leaders want equality with more developed countries, and quickly. They are well aware that with a limited budget and a growing but slender tree of higher education, progress is going to be wearisomely slow if they rely only on their own resources and conventional methods. Help is indeed offered from outside to supplement their resources; but educational orthodoxy seems often to be standing in the way of accepting it. For if the highest qualifications are insisted upon for entry into higher education overseas, they have not enough students qualified to take up the outside offers after filling their own university.

They see three possible short cuts. The first is to substitute experience for educational certificates, and to up-grade adults. The second is to accept a shorter and simpler training for those professional tasks, such as that of the rural doctor, which can in fact be well, if not perfectly, done at that level. The third is to find entry to university courses for boys and girls who do not come up to the academic standards of Higher School Certificate, and this they can do in North America and elsewhere, if not in Britain. All these aids are going to be used vigorously, whatever the academics may say. It is right that they should be; for societies rich in education and strongly trade unionised have a marked tendency to raise entry qualifications and barriers and to prolong training, partly to raise their standards still higher, partly to maintain the monopoly of established crafts and professions. Very great care is needed to distinguish those skills where the most thorough training is indeed essential—for the bridge must not collapse, nor the public service seize up—and those where something simpler will do. In Britain, the local authority officer who finds foster-parents for children must have a Social Science diploma; in Africa this would be the the greatest nonsense. On the whole, there has been a little too much pedantic insistence on 'qualifications' in Africa by expatriates, though with the best motives. Quality matched to the real requirements of the actual job in its local circumstances should be the only real test; in some cases it must still be the highest quality.

As to individual feeling, it is easy to describe with a smile the 'prestige' of the 'been-to' and deplore the efforts of individual, poorly qualified Africans to make their way overseas. Emlyn Williams, son of a poor Welsh family, described most movingly his enormous excitement as a single devoted teacher began to coach him specially at school, until at last the unbelievable dream of a scholarship to Oxford became at first conceivable, then true. How much more exciting must it have been—indeed must it still be—for an African child, moving from thatched hut to thatched primary school, to the bigger Mission School with science laboratories and library, to see suddenly the chance of London or Princeton, not only the chance to move among the lords of the world and of the mind (as Emlyn Williams saw Oxford) but to see at their source civilizations which in Africa seemed to be endowed with such authority, knowledge and power. These are not ignoble dreams. Certainly, their realization must be earned: Africans are usually prepared to work very hard to earn them. On our side in England, when all the reservations about official needs and proper qualifications have been made, a warm and generous welcome to the student who gets through to us, and a helping hand to remedy his shortcomings is surely needed. In future, as the omens are today, his own society will make it more and more difficult for the undeserving or ill-equipped to go abroad. There is a balance to be struck between a proper insistence on standards, on policy, on proper use of manpower and finance (with which earlier chapters of this study have been mainly concerned) and a certain tolerance and generosity, which will wink an eye at the regulation on behalf of some young students who have set out on the adventure of education.

In East Africa, by far the largest problem will be to find some form of continued education or training for the huge numbers of children who will soon be completing their primary course and will find no place in a grammar school. This is urgent for the Asians now; and it will become urgent for Africans in two or three years' time when primary begins to end at the age of thirteen or even twelve. In country areas, if school or training for practical life could be given even one day a week for two or three years this would help to bridge the gap between the child and the man. In towns, where there is no family land where the boy can usefully help, but only the streets, something more may be needed. This is beyond the scope of this enquiry: it is mentioned only because it dwarfs every other educational issue.

Clearly, the second main problem is in the expansion of full-time secondary education. It is, indeed, proceeding fast, though not fast enough to maintain a 10 per cent entry from primary schools by 1965. Money and teachers are needed; the teachers, for another four or five years, must be mainly expatriate. Here is the best help and the best investment which we can give.

It is only after some secondary education that the question of accepting and aiding African students overseas really arises. When a boy or girl has completed twelve years of education (it may be eleven soon, when the primary course is shortened), what next?

In broad outline, the picture is fairly clear. The stream of secondary leavers splits into three branches. The academically best are bound for a university. They may go via the Sixth Form in East Africa and thence to a degree either at home or overseas; or a few may go direct to high grade American colleges for a four year course.

The middle stream—those with Division III or lower II passes —will mainly go to vocational training in East Africa—to government (central or agricultural or medical extension), to teacher training, to the Police and other public services, including local government, to private commerce and industry, to a technical college, in East Africa or possibly abroad. Some, however, may go to the lesser American colleges and elsewhere overseas where they can find an entry. They should form a most important cadre at the lower professional and technical level.

The third stream, who are the School Certificate failures, will go to a lower level of the same range of on-training, finding themselves at the third level of extension work, in clerical training and the like. It may be that in the future this smaller group of School Certificate failures in grammar schools will find, in company with many others, a better chance of development in a 'modern' type of school with more practical and less academic emphasis—one 'Day Secondary School' in Kenya (Chavakali, Nyanza) is experimenting with a mixed school where practical workshop training co-exists with the struggle for School Certificate.

In terms of manpower requirements, East Africa can absorb all (and more) of the graduates it can produce. The East African University in turn can absorb all the Higher School Certificate passes which are in view for some years ahead, and overseas colleges can easily absorb both those who fail in HSC and some who never entered the course. Between the local and overseas effort, the urgent need for graduates should be met, save for graduate teachers; but this is a large gap.

At the next level, East Africa can absorb into good training all the SC passes, aided by some specialist finishing overseas; indeed there will be a shortage for some years if the full demand for teachers is taken into account.

In this situation, where the availability of training or higher education in East Africa matches the output of students from secondary schools able to benefit from it, the analysis in chapter VI suggests seven points where overseas training or education may still be needed and valued:

1. Adults.
2. Those who temporarily fall out of the educational stream and wish to re-enter it.
3. In special forms of training, such as pharmacy or dentistry.

All these will be dwindling demands, for adults suitable for upgrading are limited in number and will in the main find a suitable course in East Africa; fewer will fall off the ladder of advance; some of the special subjects now unavailable will soon be provided.

4. Men who need a specialized course after East African training (e.g. in range management, or in certain specialized industrial and technical fields).
5. Secondary leavers below HSC standard, capable of benefitting from further *general* education.
6. Students in technical subjects who cannot enter the three technical institutes in East Africa.
7. Graduates for post-graduate research or higher study.

Categories 3, 4 and 7 are likely to continue as groups needing overseas courses for several years. Some special emphasis may also be put on the needs of Asians who may find that the policies of African governments or their own weak position as a small minority forces them increasingly to look overseas for continued education and training.

In numerical terms, it may be a reasonable guess that about 1,200 students overseas at one time would be about the level for Uganda and Tanganyika, perhaps 1,800 or 2,000 for Kenya[1]—a total of 4,000 to 4,500, distributed between Britain, USA, India, Western Europe, Israel, the Commonwealth, the Middle East and the Iron Curtain countries, with the weight of numbers declining in roughly that order. As the years go on, the weight of students will also move towards post-graduate and special technical work and away from the lower levels of GCE(A) and the like. Some estimates of the real costs of having overseas students in British institutions will be given in the companion volume to this study; but Britain should certainly

[1] See chapter VII, p. 90.

be able to absorb comfortably at least half of the 4,000 East Africans, even allowing for the students from West and Central Africa, the Caribbean and Asia, which are a heavier load.

This account of the gaps in East Africa which overseas training might fill, by type of student and by number, has tacitly assumed that where provision does exist in East Africa, it is of proper quality. This assumption needs a little examination. It can be said with some assurance that provision in the university colleges is of high quality, both in teaching, buildings, equipment, food and general environment. These university colleges are in most respects on a scale of expense which far richer countries would gladly accept. It is the second-level institutions which need a closer look—secondary schools, technical colleges, agricultural training centres, teacher training colleges and similar units.

The transitional and mixed quality of physical conditions in the schools has been mentioned in chapter I. In a way, this mixture of simplicity and modernity does make a bridge between the Africa of subsistence farming and low income and the Africa of the modern sector, with its laboratories and engineering workshops. Up to Form 4, with gradual improvements in the less favoured schools, there is not much to criticize, and much to praise; possibly the lack of a good library reading room is the worst single feature. It is depressing to walk through school dormitories out of class room hours and find boys or girls lying on their beds for lack of a good reading room, or playing pop tunes among the dining room trestles and benches, with the smells (and even scraps) of food too much in evidence.

The conditions in post-secondary training centres, and particularly those run by government for agricultural, teacher and other vocational training are more open to serious comment in some cases. If the training to diploma level is to be in some Degree recognized and aided by the university, and carry both prestige and career prospects which are not too far below that of a degree course, then some of these institutions (Bukalasa Agricultural College is certainly one) will have to move away from a tradition which is well below that of the best secondary schools from which their 18- or 20-year old students are recruited. A diet of maize meal, squalid and overcrowded dining halls, sub-barrack room dormitories, inadequate light and space for study or recreation in a latitude where it is dark by 7.0 p.m. all the year round—these conditions are simply not good enough for young men who have a serious syllabus to master, an important job to do, and a need for self-respect and even some privacy.

It is partly the policy of carrying what should be major training institutions on a departmental budget (subject to perennial economy campaigns and conflicting claims) which results in these financially starved conditions. This policy has also a serious effect on the quality of teaching. Departmental staff are 'posted' to a training centre, whether they have any experience of teaching or any training as teachers or not. In many cases the Principal of the institution has no choice of staff—they are requisitioned by him and posted to him. In consequence, not only is the turnover too high, but the college itself never gains the tradition and standing of an autonomous educational institution. In many cases, these centres would surely do better with their own Board of Governors, with their own budget, and with their own responsibility for recruiting and selecting staff.[1] It should not be impossible to retain—which is certainly essential— a close liaison with the field staff and the central Department, without this bureaucratic control.

In the trade schools and technical colleges, it is again the training of technical teachers which has been missing. If these institutions, of which the senior ones are well equipped, are to move from older African standards to standards of fully modern technology, it is essential that staff should be fully trained in teaching methods. Aid in establishing a technical teacher training college for East Africa, as a joint enterprise, might well be a valuable British move.

In the secondary schools themselves teaching standards naturally vary widely. The bane of government schools is the 'general post' of staff which is constantly in progress. To find a school starting a new year with 5 or 6 out of 13 staff new was not at all uncommon. This can be tolerated, at a pinch, in the lower forms. But Sixth Form work does demand continuity of the principal staff, and can be ruined by frequent changes. Science teaching, too, is still shaky, for lack of staff: in three schools we found a Headmaster distraught for lack of a single biologist to teach his School Certificate science stream.

In the Mission schools, things may be better or worse. In the older larger schools staff stay longer and are usually of good quality. In some of the smaller schools, nobly manned by relatively inexperienced lay brothers, or preoccupied with sectarian concerns, the result can be more well-intentioned than wellrun. Africans, in their present mood, are very far indeed from showing a responsive gratitude to religious orders or any other group who have come from overseas to bring them education. On the contrary, they are highly critical of their professional competence and do not hesitate to show it by complaints and strikes against individual teachers— —criticism of teachers was running a close second to food as a

---

[1] A good deal of progress has been made in setting up Boards of Governors for secondary schools and teacher training colleges; this could well be extended to other vocational institutes and colleges.

pretext for the wave of strikes in secondary schools in 1961 and 1962. Some of the American teachers, recruited under the Teachers for East Africa scheme, were much disillusioned by this attitude (combined with the students' insistence on close adherence to the examination syllabus). African students, obsessed by the vital importance of an SC pass to their whole future career (who can blame them?) were particularly apt to attack the Americans as 'not knowing the British system'. This unfortunate situation could have serious results, in causing Americans not to renew their contracts and in spreading disillusion among potential American recruits to the scheme in the United States.

Finally, as to syllabus and standards, there might be much to be said about 'Africanising' the primary syllabus in some degree, and about devising a syllabus for a new class of 'modern' secondary education when it can be afforded; these issues are outside our scope. In the present secondary and technical institutions, nothing radical can or should be done, at least while the schools stick to some recognizable international standards. No doubt on the Arts side, history and geography could be more African in content; but in the Sciences the basic equipment of thought and knowledge is the same all over the world.

The real issue, and very real danger, lies in standards. Violent and sustained political pressure can lead (as it has done in some South-East Asian countries) to a vast expansion of free secondary education, without the supply of proper teachers. The next stage is a huge failure rate in university entrance; the next, a demand, perhaps conceded, to lower university entrance standards; the next, a university crammed with students unable to follow the courses or attain their degree; at last, the point is reached where the offer of scholarships overseas *cannot be accepted*, because too few students exist capable of entering an overseas course. The University of Rangoon has been through this process. By 1959 only 3 per cent of 100,000 candidates for matriculation were able to pass; 60 per cent of students who did enter the University were failing to pass their course examination;[1] standards reached such a low pitch that the Government of Burma was unable to find qualified students to take up the very modest programme of fifty overseas scholarships offered. This melancholy sequence could very easily happen in Africa; and the point to emphasize is that the downward slide does not start inside the university, but in the deterioration of an over-expanded secondary education which in time pulls the university down to its own level. It is this danger which has made those who are concerned for the future of East Africa so nervous of relaxing secondary

[1] See Hla Myint, 'The Universities of S.E. Asia and Economic Development', *Pacific Affairs*, Vol. 35, No. 2, 1962.

standards or of undermining the Sixth Form work which, more than any other factor, is already vitalizing and up-grading secondary education and saving it from the narrowest instructional struggle for School Certificate passes. Impatience to get more students into university institutions before they are ready for it can topple the whole educational structure.

It is, however, important to balance this insistence on at least one stream of the highest quality by recognizing that a safety valve must be provided to meet the pressure for more higher education, whether by up-grading second-level institutions to university diploma standing, as is suggested here, or by new means, possibly analogous to the American 'Liberal Arts College'.

The implications for the programmes of overseas bursaries and the acceptance of students are clear. There is, and will be, a need in particular subjects and categories. But generosity can be misplaced. Any encouragement to unqualified students on a large scale (there must be room for a little generosity to exceptional individuals) is only liable to upset the educational effort and the incentives which sustain it overseas. In so far as East African governments are now seeking to direct and control the movement of students overseas, and on lines which protect their own educational structure and fit their manpower requirements, it behoves us in Britain to support them and to co-operate with them in making these controls effective and beneficial.

As a last word, it may be worth while emphasizing once again the warning from countries which have had not one or two but ten or fifteen years of independence. Such countries, yielding to the demand for massive university expansion, have found themselves with far more university graduates, sometimes of poor quality, than their slowly-growing modern sector can employ. BAs and even engineers are out of work or driving taxis. This has meant heavy expenditure which would have been far better directed to productive investment or the usual economy. East Africa still has high standards, and a reasonable balance between education and economic growth. It would be throwing away a vital asset to lose this balance simply through impatience at the purely temporary manpower shortage in 1963.

INDEX

ACCOUNTANCY, 31, 40, 50, 51, 53, 102: accountants, 34, 51, 101
Addis Ababa, 83
Administration, xvi, 38; training in, 36, 37, 40, 47–8
African—American Institute, 85
African District Council, 15, 71, 88
African Girls' High School, Kikuyu, 26
Africanisation, xii, xv, 14, 15–16, 34–5, 36, 37, 38, 45, 46, 47–8, 50, 57, 58, 65, 69, 74, 76, 78, 79, 80, 83, 85, 87, 89
African Scholarship Program of American Universities, 85–6, 88, 98
Aga Khan, H. H. the, 18: H. H. the Aga Khan School, Uganda, 26
A I D (Agency for International Development), 85–6
Agricultural Institute, Uganda, 102
Agricultural Services, 60, 62, 66–7
Agriculture, 6, 7, 8; European, xv; training in, xi, 12, 13, 15, 28–9, 35, 36, 37, 41, 44–6, 72, 98, 99; training centres for, 8–9, 110; Asians and, 38, 102
Agriculture Departments, 15, 46
Alliance High School, Kenya, 26, 81
America, 38, 74, 80, 91 (see United States)
American (a) aid, 9, 16; (b) educational grants, 14, 81, 83, 85–6, 87, 88, 95, 96, 104; (c) universities, xii, 15, 79, 91, 98, 106, 107, 108, 109, 112
Apprenticeships, xiv, 51, 98, 102
'Aptitude-Testing' Unit, Kenya, 35
Arabs, 23, 92, 94
Arapai, Uganda, 44
Architecture, 40, 41, 50: architects, 51
Armed Services, recruitment by, 15
Artisans, 11, 19, 20, 58; training of, 10, 29–31, 34, 48, 50, 51, 52, 53; wages of, 103, 104
Arucha, Tanganyika, 33, 71
Ashby Report (1960), xiv
Asians, Africans and, xv-xvi, 20–1; schools for, 3–4, 18, 26, 49, 92–4; and education, 18–19, 64, 81, 89, 107, 109; opportunities for, 19–20, 38, 58, 67, 102–3; Europeans and, xvi, 20; future of, 21–2; in commerce, 35, 51; in agriculture, 38, 102; as lawyers, 61; as doctors, 61, 65; scholarships for, 92–3
Australia, 85, 96

BALHAM AND TOOTING TECHNICAL COLLEGE, 84
Banks, 20, 35, 52, 100, 101
Barclays D.C.O., 52
Bata Shoe Co., 34, 52
Bath, England, 102
Beit-el-Ras, 92
Belgian Congo, 86
Bell Lane Institute, England, 84
Binns Report, 4
Boards of Governors for schools, 111
Bonding system, West Africa, 89
Book-keeping, 32, 33
Britain, xiii, xiv, xvi, 6, 7, 38, 74, 79, 81, 87, 102, 107, 109 (see Great Britain; United Kingdom)
British Commonwealth, xii, 81, 96, 109
British Council, 14, 41, 81, 84, 87
British Council for Technical Education and Training in Overseas Countries, 31–2
British universities, xii, xiii, 7, 8, 10, 17, 75, 79, 95, 97, 102, 106, 107
Broadcasting, 100
Brooke Bond Tea Co., 53
Budo College, Uganda, 26, 74
Building, trades, 6, 7, 14, 19, 29–30; training for, 28, 31, 32, 102
Bukalasa Agricultural College, Uganda, 44, 45, 110
Baloba Junior Secondary Teacher Training College, Uganda, 102
Burma, xi, xiii, 112
Busoga College, Uganda, 26
Bwira School, Mwanza, Tanganyika, 101

CAIRO, 83
Caltex Oil Co., 52
Cambridge Overseas School Certificates, 3, 5, 11, 92, 101; Higher Certificates, 93
Canada, 80, 96
Central Africa, 40, 86, 110
Central East African Assembly, 102
Ceylon, 96
Chagga coffee-growers, 29
Chande Industries, 53
Chavakali, Nyanza, 108
Chemistry, 9, 32, 39: chemists, 20, 34
China, 16, 86
City and Guilds Institute, 14, 31, 32–3
Civil engineering, 12, 31, 41
Civil Service, 14, 16, 18, 20, 21, 37, 38, 61, 68–9, 103; training for, xi, 72, 98
Civil Service Training Centre, Tanganyika, 47

Clerks, xi, 15, 19–20, 21, 48; clerical work, 35, 47, 99; training for, 32, 36, 42, 47–8, 51, 52–3, 102
Coast Trade School, 29
Coffee Plantations Co., 53
College of Agricultural Technology, 76
College of Social Studies, Kikuyu, 72
Colonial Development and Welfare, 9, 81
Colonial Office, Britain, 87
Colwyn Bay Wireless Office, 84
Commerce, xvi, 19–20, 21; training in, 12, 13, 29, 31, 32, 34–5, 51–3, 72; recruitment to, 35, 100, 108
Commonwealth Relations Office, Britain, 87
Commonwealth Scholarship Plan, 96
Communist countries, 16, 41, 81, 83, 109
Community Development, training in, 13, 28–9, 35, 37, 48; service, 36
Companies, training given by, 15, 34, 52–3; recruitment by, 15, 53 (see Commerce)
'Comprehensive' schools, xi
Co-operative Development Department, 100
Co-operation, training in, 13, 28, 35, 36–7, 79, 100; school of, 13
Co-operative (a) Service, 36, 100 (b) Union, 33; co-operatives, xvi, 29, 53
Corvallis, Oregon, 85
Council of Ministers, Kenya, 88
Crafts, rural, 6, 28–9
Curle, Professor Adam, x
Customs and Excise, 35

DAB PIENAAR MEMORIAL FUND, 95
Dar-es-Salaam, 52; Technical Institute, 14, 31, 32, 50, 100; University College, 16, 38, 40–1, 100, 102; Asian school at, 26; Prison, training at, 29; Government training centre at, 37, 47; tobacco factory at, 52
Day schools, 3, 18, 19; 'day secondary school', 108
Delemere High School, Nairobi, 17
Denmark, 45, 100
Dentistry, 19, 42, 47, 51, 76, 109
Department of Politics, Uganda, 47
Department of Technical Co-operation, Britain, 87
Development craft centres, Uganda, 28
Dietetics, 51
District Officers, 47–8
Doctors, xvi, 19, 21, 51, 60, 61, 103
Domestic (a) science, 13, 29, 31, 40, 41, 101 (b) training, 28
Duchess of Gloucester Girls' School, Kenya, 26
Duke of Gloucester School, Kenya, 26
Duke of York School, Kenya, 17, 25

EAST AFRICA HIGH COMMISSION, 13
East African Airways, 34
East African Common Services, 35
East African Posts and Telecommunications, 34, 52
East African Power and Lighting, 34, 52
East African Railways & Harbours, 15, 18, 34, 52, 67, 87, 95, 100
East African Tobacco Co., 34, 52
Eastern Nigeria, xi
Education, higher, xiii, 10, 72, 81–2, 94, 106, 113; intermediate, 15; for Europeans, 4, 17–18; training in, 13 (see teacher training); for Asians, 18–19, 64, 81, 89, 107, 109 (see Overseas; Primary; Secondary; Technical; University)
Educational grants, 71, 73 (see Scholarships)
Educational Strategy for Developing Societies, x
Education Departments, 15
Egerton College, Kenya, 45
Egypt, 16, 41, 83
Eldoret, Kenya, Secondary School at, 17; Trade School at, 29, 30
Electrical engineering, training in, 12, 14, 31, 33, 40; engineers, 67
Electrical trades, 14, 30; electricians, 29, 30
Electronics, 42, 76
Embu, Kenya, 44
Engineering, ix, 14, 31, 38, 41, 50, 102–3; training in, 12, 32, 33, 52; trades, 14, 30; engineers, xvi, 19, 34, 51, 60, 67
English, as medium of instruction, 4–6, 19; training in, 8, 32–3, 39, 40
Ethiopia, 16, 41, 81, 83, 86, 96
Europe, travel in, 77–8
Europeans, replacement of, xv, 58, 65, 83; and agriculture, xv; and Asians, xv, 20; and education, 4, 17–18, 81; and Africans, 15, 20; School Certificates passed by, 19, 63–4; prestige of, 21; schools for, 25–6, 49; in commerce, 35; employment of, 58, 103; scholarships, for, 92–5 (see Expatriates)
Evans, P. C. C., 6, 7
Evening Institutes, 71; evening classes, 32
Expatriates, as teachers, 3, 9, 19, 33, 68–9, 73, 108; as employers, 5; Europeans in Kenya likely to be treated as, 17; replacement of, 57, 65, 83, 104; as 'experts', 65, 103; and insistence on 'qualifications', 69, 107; and training of Africans overseas, 87 (see Europeans)
Extension staff, 36, 42, 58, 99

'FALL OUT' IN SCHOOLS, 10, 24–5, 27
Farmers' Training Centres, 79
Ford Foundation, 32, 67
Forestry Departments, 13: forest rangers, training for, 35, 48
Fort Hare University, 81

GAILEY AND ROBERTS, MESSRS., 34, 52
Game Departments, 13, 35, 48, 99
Gandhi Memorial Trust, 14, 95
Gayaza High School, Buganda, 26, 101–2
G.C.E. (General Certificate of Education), 27–8, 36, 50, 63, 64, 101; at Ordinary level, xi, 33, 99; at Advanced level, xii, 31, 33, 50, 80, 91, 102, 109; courses for, 98, 99
Geography, 32, 33, 39, 40
Geological Survey Department, 46, 100
Ghana, xii, xv
Girl Guide Association, 102
Girls, schools for, 3, 17, 26; training for, 13, 28, 38; school certificates passed by, 19; opportunities for, 99, 101–2 (see Women)
Goans, xvi, 23, 25, 84, 92
Government service, 91
Government Teacher Training College, Kyanbogo, 33
Graduates, 61, 65, 90, 95, 108; mass-produced, xi, xiv, xv; in commerce, 34; as teachers, 49–50, 60, 68, 99, 108; in industry, 99
Grammar schools, xii, xiii, 107
Grants for education, 71, 73 (see Scholarships)
Great Britain, xii, 21, 113 (see Britain)
Gujeratis, xvi, 20

HARPER - WOODHEAD REPORT (1958), 18–19
Higher (National) Certificates, 31
Higher School Certificates, xii, 3, 4, 25–6, 27, 28, 38, 42, 50, 53, 61, 63–4, 67, 69, 70–1, 72, 73, 86; courses for, 71–5, 104; candidates for, 93
High-Level Manpower in East Africa, 57
Hindus, xvi
Hocking, W. E. (quoted), ix
Holland, 45, 79, 81
Hospital Hill School, Nairobi, 17
Hunter, G. and L. (quoted), 12–13
Hunter, G. and Harbison, F. H. (quoted), 57

IFUNDA TRADE SCHOOL, TANGANYIKA, 30
Ihungu School, Bukoba, Tanganyika, 26

India, 16, 21, 41, 45, 67, 81–2, 83, 86, 94, 96, 99, 109; Indians, xvi
Indonesia, xi, xv
Industrial Art, training for, 33
Industry, training for, xi, 12, 34–5, 51–3, 71, 72; recruitment into, 38, 98–9, 100, 108
Institutes of Technology, 76
'Intermediate' schools, Kenya, 3, 10, 15
International Institute of Education, New York, 85
Iringa, Tanganyika, 17
Ismailis, 18, 95
Israel, 16, 45, 81, 86, 109
Italy, 45, 81, 95

JEANES SCHOOLS, KENYA, 37
Jinja, Uganda, 34, 52, 71; Jinja Textiles, Co., 34
Journalism, 51
'Junior Colleges', 71, 76, 80
'Junior secondary' schools, Uganda, 3, 24

KABAKA OF BUGANDA, 14
Kabete Technical and Trade School, Kenya, 13, 29, 30
Kagumo Teacher Training College, Kenya, 104
Kakamega School, Kenya, 26
Kampala Technical Institute, Kyambogo, 13, 31, 33, 50; Technical School, 33
Kamusinga School, Kenya, 26
Kangaru School, Embu, Kenya, 26
Kansas, U.S.A., 45, 85
Karinjee School, Tanga, 26
Kenya, educational system of, 3; English used for teaching in schools in, 5; poverty in, 8; examination results in, 10–11, 19, 23–4, 26–7; departmental training courses in, 12–14, 44–6; technical training in, 12, 14, 26, 28–9, 31–2, 35; rapid advance in, 15–16; Europeans in, 17–18; Asians in, 18, 22; schools in 23–4; Government bursaries in, 87–8, 92–4
Kenya Farmers' Association bursaries, 96
Kenya Farmers' Union, 53
Kenya High School for Girls, 17, 25
Kenya Institute of Administration, 16, 37, 47–8, 49
Kenya Overseas Scholarship Advisory Committee, 88–9
Kenya Polytechnic, Nairobi, 14, 18, 31, 67
Kenyatta, Jomo, 81
Kericho, Kenya, 71
Kikuyu, Kenya, 72
Kilembe Copper Mine, Uganda, 53
Kisii School, Uganda, 26

Kishbi School, Uganda, 26
Kisumu, Kenya, 32, 71; Asian School at, 18, 26
Kiswahili language, 4, 5
K.N.C.U. (Kilimanjaro Native Co-operative Union) College of Commerce, Moshi, 29, 31, 33, 53
Kololo School, Uganda, 26
Kyambogo, Uganda, Technical Institute at, 33, 49

LABOUR DEPARTMENT, KENYA, 29
Lancaster House Conference (1959), 14
Land and Surveys Department, 35, 46, 48
Langata, Kenya, 34, 52
Law, 21, 38, 40, 41, 102; lawyers, xvi, 19, 51, 60, 61, 103
'Liberal Arts Colleges', 76, 113
Limuru, Kenya, 52; school at, 17
'Literacy' schooling, 6–8
Liverpool, 102
Local Government, 28, 37, 47–8, 108; training in, 35
'Localisation' courses, 31
Loughborough College, 33–4, 87

MACHAKOS TRADE SCHOOL, KENYA, 29
Makerere College, Uganda, 10, 11, 14, 15, 17, 25, 37, 38–9, 40–2, 46, 47, 49, 51, 65, 69, 73, 74, 93, 97, 100, 102: Makerere College School, 26
Malaya, xi, 96
Malta, 96
Manpower needs, xiv, xvi, 23, 28, 57–69, 74, 78, 89, 90, 107, 108, 113
Mathematics, xii, 6, 32, 33, 39, 40
Mau Mau Emergency, 15, 28
Mawego Trade School, South Nyanza, 29
Mbale, Uganda, 71, 101; school at, 26; medical training at, 47, 66
Mbeya, Tanganyika, 17
Mboya, Tom, 15, 83
Mechanical engineering, 12, 31, 32, 33, 40, 102
Mechanics, 29–30
Medical Colleges, 76
Medical Departments, 15, 100
Medical Service, 61, 65–6; training for, xi, 9, 12, 13, 35, 36, 37–8, 46–7, 72, 98
Medical Training Centre, Kenya, 12, 13
Medicine, 21, 38, 102
Metallurgy, 51, 61
Michelin Tyre Factory, 33
Middle East, students in, 109
'Middle' schools, Tanganyika, 3
Mining engineering, 42, 51, 76
Ministry of Labour, Kenya, 35

Ministry of Works, 13, 48
Missions, 6, 14, 82, 84, 87, 88, 101, 107, 111
Mombasa, schools at, 17, 18, 30; Institute of Muslim Education, 30, 31, 32; Shell Refinery at, 52
Morogoro College, Tanganyika, 45, 49, 85
Moscow, 83, 86
Moshi, Tanganyika, 29; school at, 26; trade school at, 30, 33
Mothers' Union, 102
Mulago Hospital, Uganda, 47
Muljibhai Madhvani School of Commerce, Kyambogo, 33
Multi-racial society, 15, 20
Munali, Northern Rhodesia, 99
Muslims, xvi, 30, 95; Muslim Institute, Mombasa, 30, 31, 32
Mwanza, Tanganyika, 71
Mzumbe Training Centre, Tanganyika, 16, 37, 47

NABBINGO GIRLS' SCHOOL, UGANDA, 26
Nabumali School, Uganda, 101
Nairobi, Kenya, 9, 18, 34, 49, 52, 67; Asian schools at, 30; Technical Institute, 31, 50
Namilyango School, Uganda, 26
National and Grindlays Bank, 52
National Assembly, Uganda, 102
National income, 59–61, 104
New Zealand, 45, 85, 96, 99
Nigeria, xii, xiv
North Africa, 86
Northern Rhodesia, xii
North Nyanza District, Kenya, 50
Nsamizi College, Uganda, 28, 37, 47
Ntare School, Uganda, 26
Nuffield Foundation, 4
Nursing, 13, 21, 38, 46, 101, 102
Nuttall, Mr. 29
Nyanza Textile Co., 53
Nyanza Trade School, 29
Nyasaland, xii, 96
Nyerere, Dr., xiv, 14, 21
Nyeri, Kenya, 71

OLD EAST AFRICA TRADING CO., 52
Old Kampala School, Uganda, 26
Oliver, Roland, 6
Ordinary (National) Certificates 31, 33
Ottoman Bank, 52
Overseas education, x–xi, xii, xiii, 5, 6, 14–15, 16, 21, 28, 37, 38, 41, 42, 46, 47, 49, 50, 51, 52–3, 63, 64, 66, 70–113
Oxford Conference on Tensions in Development (1961), 23, 41

PAKISTAN, 21, 45, 94, 96: Pakistanis, xvi
Passports, 87, 88, 89
Peking, 16, 86
Personal preference in education, 97–105
Pharmacy, ix, 42, 51, 66, 79, 109; pharmacists, 47, 103
Philippines, xi
Physics, 9, 32, 40
Physiotherapy, 46, 51, 66, 102; physiotherapists, 47
Poland, 86
Police, training for, 9, 12–13, 32, 35, 36, 108; recruitment by, 15, 99
Post-graduate study, xii, 46, 61, 70, 77, 80, 91, 95–6, 99, 105, 109
Posts and Telecommunications, 13, 15, 32, 44–5, 101
Post-secondary students, xi, xii, 42
Preliminary Scholastic Aptitude Tests, 86
Pre-university courses, 10, 72–4, 91, 97
Primary (a) education, 3–5, 10, 15, 17, 103; expansion of, xi, 18, 107 (b) schools, 3, 8, 9; pressure on, x
Prince of Wales School, Kenya, 17, 25
Princetown Conference (1960), 69, 84
Private Schools, 4
Provincial Councils, 71
Psychology, 39, 51
'Public Schools', 4, 17
Public services, xv, xvi, 14, 18, 20, 21
Public utilities, 34, 38, 51, 91, 98, 103
Public Works Department, 33, 35, 38; Engineering School, Kampala, 33

RACIAL DISCRIMINATION, xv–xvi, 18, 103
Radiography, 46, 47, 66
Radio mechanics, 30, 32
Railways, 32, 35, 101
Range management, 79, 109
Rattansi Trust Bursaries, 95
Residential schools, 3, 17, 71
Rhodesia and Nyasaland, 96
Roman Catholics, 6, 73–4
Royal College, Nairobi, 9, 11, 12, 13, 14, 38, 41–2, 46, 48, 50, 51, 53, 67, 74, 98, 100
Royal College of Mines, Loughborough, 87
Royal Technical College, Nairobi, 9, 11, 12, 13, 14, 16, 17, 31, 41, 93, 95, 102
Rural crafts, training in, 28–9
Rural Medical Practitioners, 42, 47, 66, 100, 106
Ruskin, John, 7
Russia, 41, 77–8

ST. ANDREW'S SCHOOL, MINAKI 25, 26

St. Francis School, Pugu, 25, 26
St. Michael & St. George School, Iringa, 17, 25
Sandhurst, 99
Scholarships and bursaries, x, xiii, 14, 21, 28, 77, 81–105, 112–3
School buildings, 8–9, 19, 110
Schools, secondary, x–xl, 3, 8–9, 17, 18, 43, 49, 90–1, 110, 111–2; 'comprehensive', xi; primary, 3, 8, 9; day, 3, 18, 19, 108; residential, 3, 17, 71; integration in, 4, 17, 23, 25, 26, 49–50; intermediate, 10; secondary modern, 18; strikes in, 30, 111–2
Science, 6, 7–8, 9, 10, 12, 31, 32, 33, 61–2, 67–8, 107, 111, 112; training in, 33: scientists, 21, 60
Secondary (a) education, xv, 3–4, 10, 15, 63, 70, 73, 103; expansion of, x–xi, 16, 27, 68, 105, 108 (b) schools, x–xi, 3, 8–9, 17, 18, 43, 49, 90–1, 110, 111–2; pressure on, x. 15, 24–5, 27, 57, 107; secondary modern, 18; Asians and, 19; technical, 30–1, 33, 43
Shell Oil Co., 52
Shimo-la-Tewa School, Coast, Kenya, 26
Sherborne School for Girls, England, 102
Sigalagala Trade School, Kenya, 50
Sikhs, xvi, 20
Singer Sewing Machine, Co., 13
Siriba, Nyanza, Kenya, 44, 45; Teacher Training College at, 104
Sisal Plantation Companies, 53
Sixth Forms, xi, xii, 5, 9, 17, 25–6, 38, 67, 71, 72–5, 80, 97, 98–9, 100, 108, 111, 112
Smith McKenzie, Messrs., 52
Social science, xii, 107: social welfare, 101–2
South Africa, 17; universities in, 95; High Commission Territories, 86
South African Institute of Personel Administration, 35
South-East Asia, xii, 112
Southern Highlands, Tanganyika, 30
South Nyanza, Kenya, 29
Spain, 81
Standard Bank, 52
Stenographers, xiv, 13, 32, 33
Strathmore College, Nairobi, 26, 73–4
Study Abroad, 82
Sukarno, President, xv
Survey, 12, 40, 41, 48, 50; surveyors, 48, 51, 100
Survey and Lands Department, 35, 46, 48
Swynnerton Plan, Kenya, 15

TABORA GIRLS' SCHOOL, 25, 26

Tabora Government Secondary School, 25, 26, 99–101
Tanga, Tanganyika, 26, 71
Tanganyika, educational system of, 3–4; poverty in, 8; examination results, in, 11, 26, 27–8; technical training in, 14, 29, 30, 32–3; rapid progress in, 15; schools in, 17, 23, 25; Asians in, 18; departmental training in, 44
Tanganyika African National Union, 15
Tanganyika Electric Supply Co., 52
Tawney, Richard Henry, 7
Teachers, African, 3–4, 5, 7, 9–10, 49–50; expatriate, 3, 9, 33, 68–9, 73, 108; supply of, 62, 68–9, 109; technical courses for, 30, 111; scholarships for, 93–4, 96; graduates as, 49–50, 60, 68, 99, 108
Teachers for East Africa scheme, 69, 112
Teacher training, xi, 5, 12, 35, 36, 37, 38, 48–50, 80, 98, 99, 100, 101, 108; centres, 8–9; colleges, 104, 110
Technical (a) institutes and colleges, xii, 31–4, 35, 43, 71–2, 91, 108, 111 (b) training, xiii–xiv, 17–18, 20, 28–9 (c) schools, 12–14 (d) teacher training college, 111
Technicians, xiv, 14, 19, 21, 36, 46, 51, 52, 72, 103
Telecommunications, 31, 51
Tengeru Training Centre, Tanganyika, 37, 44
The Missionary Factor in East Africa, 6
Thika Trade School, Kenya, 29, 71
Tobias, G. (quoted), 30
Tororo School, Uganda, 101
Trade Schools, 8, 10, 12–14, 15, 29–31, 35, 50, 103, 111
Trade testing, 29, 30, 35
Training centres, 9, 12–13, 29
Twentsche Co., 52
Typists, xiv, 32

UGANDA, educational system in, 3; schools in, 4, 17, 23, 24–5; poverty in, 8; examination results in, 11, 24, 26, 27–8; technical training in, 14, 28, 30–1, 33–4, rapid advance in, 14–15; Asians in, 19; departmental training in, 44–6
Uganda Company, 53
Uganda Development Corporation, 53
Uganda Electricity Board, Jinja, 34, 52
Uganda Sugar Plantations, 53
Uganda Teachers' Association, 102
Ukuriguru, Tanganika, 44
U N E S C O, 31 33–4, 82
Unga Flour Mills, 53
United Arab Republic, 81, 86

United Kingdom, 41, 80, 82, 54, 87–8, 96 (see Britain); aid given by, 14, 33, 41, 81, 84, 87
United Nations' Special Fund, 31
United States of America, 21, 41, 45, 77–9, 82, 83–4, 85, 87–8, 97, 99, 100, 102 (see America)
United States Information Service, 85, 95
Universities (a) Bristol, 102 (b) Cambridge (Girton College) 102 (c) East Africa, 14, 38, 75, 91, 108; Council of, 57 (d) Harvard, 79 (e) London, 8, 10, 107 (f) Oxford, 79, 107 (g) Patrice Lumumba, Moscow, 86 (h) Princeton, 107 (i) Rangoon, 112 (j) West Virginia, 83
University College, Dar-es-Salaam, 16, 38, 40–1, 100, 102
University colleges, 9, 16, 72, 82, 90, 97, 110
University education, xi–xiv, xv, 9, 16, 52, 59, 70–1, 75–6, 80, 99, 104, 108, 112, 113
Upgrading of (a) colleges, 16 (b) training institutes, 29, 35, 75–6, 80 (c) officials, 37–8, 43, 46–9, 63, 66, 91 (d) qualifications for overseas awards 104–5 (e) graduates, 106, 109 (f) secondary education, 112–3

VERNACULARS IN SCHOOLS, 4–5
Veterinary (a) science, 39, 41, 100 (b) services, 60, 66–7; training for, 12, 35, 36, 37–8, 44–8, 51, 85
Veterinary Training Institute, Entebbe, 45
Victoria League, 53
Vocational training, xi, 12–13, 59, 72, 74–5, 80, 108; departmental, 13, 35–8, 44–6, 98, 110

WAGES, 103, 104
Water Department, 13, 35, 41, 48
West Africa, 86, 89, 110
Western Europe, scholarships from, 16, 86, 109
Westernisation, 5–6
West Germany, 81
West Indies, 40, 110
Wigglesworth and Co. 52
Williams, Emlyn, 107
Williamsons Diamond Mine, 100
Women, Studies sections for, 33; training for, 29, 80 (see Girls)
Working Men's Colleges, England, 7
World Bank Mission, 23, 30, 34

Y. W. C. A., 102
Youth clubs, Kenya, 28–9

ZANZIBAR, 40

GEORGE ALLEN & UNWIN LTD
London: 40 Museum Street, WC1

Auckland: 24 Wyndham Street
Bombay: 15 Graham Road, Ballard Estate, Bombay 1
Bridgetown: P.O. Box 222
Buenos Aires: Escritorio 454–459, Florida 165
Calcutta: 17 Chittaranjan Avenue, Calcutta 13
Cape Town: 109 Long Street
Hong Kong: 44 Mody Road, Kowloon
Ibadan: P.O. Box 62
Karachi: Karachi Chambers, McLeod Road
Madras: Mohan Mansions, 38c Mount Road, Madras 6
Mexico: Villalongin 32–10, Piso, Mexico 5, D.F.
Nairobi: P.O. Box 4536
New Delhi: 13–14 Asaf Ali Road, New Delhi 1
Sao Paulo: Avenida 9 De Julho 1138–Ap. 51
Singapore: 36c Prinsep Street, Singapore 7
Sydney, N.S.W.: Bradbury House, 55 York Street
Tokyo: 10 Kanda-Ogawamachi, 3-chome, Chiyoda-Ku
Toronto: 91 Wellington Street West, Toronto 1

T.E.A.